THE MAGIC CARPET

AN ASIAN AMERICAN STORY

THE MAGIC CARPET

AN ASIAN AMERICAN STORY

BY LORETTA TAAM
AS TOLD TO ERIC LASTER

op·si·math

LOS ANGELES

op·si·math

Published by Opsimath Press
First paperback edition

ISBN 979 8 9991928 0 6
Library of Congress Control Number 2025935530

Book design by Ryan Corey

In memory of Steve,
and dedicated to my daughters with love

1

THIS WAS JUST AFTER THE WAR. I must have been about seven and we were living in Canton, in a flat owned by Auntie Fong, my father's eldest sister. We occupied the top two floors, which included the roof garden, and my mother dragged me from the flat and down the stairs to the security gate on the landing below our front door. I don't remember what had made her so angry, only that she had accused me of lying to her. I denied it and she told me to get out of the house, and when I persisted, asking her to please believe that I hadn't lied, she said I was a stubborn child who needed a good lesson and started beating me on my calves with the rattan handle of a feather duster. I begged her to stop—usually, if I admitted wrongdoing, she would. But on that day she kept hitting me, then pulled me by the arm to the security gate and locked me out and started walking up to the flat. Dizzy with pain, I held on to the iron bars, crying, and again falsely confessed, asking her to forgive me.

"Too late," she said.

She told me that she no longer wanted me as her daughter. I

sobbed and held tighter to the iron bars to keep from fainting.

My godfather, who was living with us, came out of the flat.

"Let her stay this time," he said.

My mother followed him back inside without a word. I have no idea how many minutes passed before my nanny Ah Sam came and unlocked the security gate and brought me to her own room, where she put me in her bed and gave me hot water to drink. By the afternoon, I had a fever. The next day, I was too sick to go to school, but I was relieved because there were red and purple bruises all along the back of my legs that wouldn't have been covered by my skirt.

I don't know where my father was.

Why tell of these things now? My situation is not unique. Widowed after three-and-a-half decades of marriage, death and loneliness have unsurprisingly sent my thoughts reeling back through the years. All those I've known and lost, the paths taken and avoided: it's as if, whether I will it or no, some part of me has decided that by living with them again, re-experiencing them, I can bleed melancholy like an ancient cure.

I am grieving then. For Steve. I despise myself for this, normal though it is. I can't help feeling that I'm being weak. And yet grief could be a strength, couldn't it? *I can't go on. I'll go on.* One mourns, one wallows, but the garbage still needs to be taken out and the bills paid.

In 1931, taking advantage of China's patchwork governance and the fighting between Nationalists and Communists, Japan invaded resource-rich Manchuria and set up a puppet regime. After the July 7th Incident in 1937, when unannounced military exercises led to an exchange of gunfire, the war with the Japanese escalated. My parents decided it would be safest to leave Canton, where they were living in De-Di's family home, my brother's birthplace. They fled to Hong Kong, and I was born. My godfather moved in with us and everything was relatively peaceful until the Japanese invaded in December of 1941, burning buildings to the ground, including the hospital where I'd taken my first breath. The British didn't have a military presence in Hong Kong, considering it a minor seaport, and promptly surrendered. But in early 1942, it was still possible to leave. My godfather—a man with prominent connections—decided to go to Chongqing, the temporary capital of the Nationalist government. My parents, brother, and I took a boat to Guilin, in Guangxi—a well-known scenic destination for Chinese, famed for its karst mountains and cave systems on both sides of the Li River.

Sirens were screaming and voices blared from loudspeakers, warning of approaching enemy airplanes. MPs knocked at every guest room of our hotel—bang bang! bang bang bang!—and urged people to leave. My mother helped me and my older brother to quickly dress. My father grabbed a can of soda crackers and a thermos bottle of water, and we hurried outside to join the crowds running to what served as a bomb shelter—the network of limestone caves in Guilin's Seven Star Park. In the scurry and panic to get underground,

I was very afraid of being separated from my parents. We bumped past more than a few children crying, standing still, looking all about them as if they were lost.

Packed into the Seven Star Cave with so many people, I found it difficult to breathe. To this day, I get uncomfortable in any space without a window. I suffer anxiety attacks in elevators and avoid them whenever possible.

The all-clear sounded. We jostled our way out of the cave, and I saw a dead body for the first time—several, in fact, riddled with bullet holes and lying at the foot of Guilin's city wall, where the people had tried to hide during the air raid.

We moved from the hotel into a small house near the city wall. My brother began to attend a Christian school. I started kindergarten. There was a contingent of American military in Guilin—Air Force officers, advisors, pilot trainees—and my mother and a number of Chinese ladies who spoke English were recruited to entertain them; every weekend, they went to the USO for socials, dances. My mother often came home with canned goods and cartons of cigarettes. It wasn't the worst of times, but the air raids increased. More and more, we huddled in Seven Star Cave with countless others, waiting for the all-clear to sound. More and more, we emerged to the sight of dead bodies along the city wall.

Scenic Guilin, my parents deemed, was no longer safe.

We traveled to Liuzhou, where we briefly stayed with Mr. Fok, a friend of my father's, and his family. Two other families joined us, and we all continued southwest, deeper into Guangxi. It was hot and humid. Provisions were scarce. We passed through numerous small villages and I contracted malaria, but I don't know if the disease had anything to do with my recurring nightmare—of a huge cannonball rolling toward me. I always screamed until my parents woke me up and wiped the sweat from my forehead and body.

The Japanese were ahead of us, marching to Chongqing. On the road, we saw the severed arms and legs of their victims. Once, we saw a man's head with gaps in its mouth.

"They probably took the gold teeth," I heard my father say to Mr. Fok.

It wasn't easy to communicate with villagers, as their language was different not only from Cantonese but from one village to the next. Yet wherever we went, the story was the same: the Japanese had looted storehouses, taking all the preserved pork, and raped many young women.

We had additional worries besides the Japanese. A villager warned that bandits had heard of us, a roving group of Chinese from Hong Kong, and they believed us to be rich. Bandits were notoriously crass, ignorant, violent. Stories abounded of how they kidnapped foreigners and held them for ransom, cutting off a hostage's finger or ear and sending it to negotiators to encourage that their demands be met.

To them, because we had come from Hong Kong, we were foreigners.

We settled in a village with an old watchtower, where each family had a floor: us, the Foks, and the two other families. The Japanese were a fading threat by 1945, and after living in Guangxi for three years, my parents—together with the Foks and heads of the other two families—determined that we could return home. Of course, as I had never been to Canton, I wasn't "returning" anywhere. Canton was less my "home" than Hong Kong or the village with the watchtower or even Guilin.

We rented a sampan and took the river route but didn't get far before bandits raided our boat and stole almost everything we had, even my favorite pillow—made for me when I was two years old. One of them, however, was surprisingly polite. He seemed to like my mother and gave her back a small amount of money, which we would need to reach Canton. Later, I learned that many bandits had formerly been villagers and soldiers made destitute by years of war; that disillusioned by government corruption, tired of being trampled by fate and wanting better lives, they had become bandits to assert some control over their destiny, leaving behind wives and children they hoped to see again one day. But I knew none of this then. With childish instinct, I simply tried to exploit a man's attraction to my mother.

"Can I have my pillow back?" I asked the polite bandit.

I felt my mother tense, but he laughed and gave it to me. The pillow is still with me—worn and thin, its stuffing decomposed almost to powder, the cotton case no longer white but tea-stained, mapped with traces of tears and saliva.

I once read that history is the memory of nation-states, but this is arrogant nonsense, the wishful thinking of a self-aggrandizing, momentarily powerful person. It is a statement that merely draws attention to its author's lack of humanity.

We sailed on toward "home," making short stops along the way for food. At one of these stops, we went to the marketplace and saw our personal belongings for sale; vendors had bought them from the bandits. Not wanting any trouble, we didn't complain. Our money had run out, and in order to buy something to eat, we needed to sell some of the clothes we were wearing, as well as a few blankets that hadn't been stolen. Which we did, quietly, and left.

We arrived in Canton after another couple of weeks on the river. Because my father's family home—except for the portion of it reserved for Po-Po, my widowed step-grandmother—was rented out, we moved into the flat owned by Auntie Fong. My godfather again came to live with us, bringing money.

Losing weight at the rate of ⅝ths of a pound per week, I calculate that it will take me twenty months to disappear. A full two years after Steve's death, I'll be thin enough for the Alameda winds to carry me wherever they wish. I can think of worse endings.

The garbage needs to be taken out and the bills paid, I said. So I must not want to die, otherwise why would I care? It's just that I forget to eat. But do I forget, or is it that I can never decide what I want now that I only have to cook for myself?

No courage to die, no strength to live, yet here I sit.

Guanyin, God, please help me to again find purpose in my life and be productive, or to accept merely existing, to appreciate it as one does a beautiful sunset, as not somehow disloyal to Steve's memory.

During the first two-and-a-half years I lived in Canton, malarial attacks forced me to miss enormous amounts of school. A few days nearly every week, I lay shivering and feverish under several blankets in bed, my mother regularly plying me with castor oil.

"It will clean out your system," she said.

There wasn't much to clean. I weighed forty-four pounds.

I sometimes had seizures, although, as with my cannonball nightmare, I don't know if these were caused by the disease. Possibly they were psychosomatic because every time I suffered an attack, I grew anxious about missing school—the more I was absent, the harder it was to make friends—and I hated the boredom of being stuck in bed, not getting to eat regular food. And then there were the bitter quinine pills I washed down with orange juice every day, even when I wasn't laid up. They tasted worse when I was confined to my bed.

Chinese medicine is based on hot and cold. If these are in balance, one is in good health, and practitioners of Chinese medicine seek to balance the hot and cold of a patient's internal organs. Which is what my step-grandmother tried to do. Hearing that dog meat cured malaria, she went out to the countryside and bought some.

"But I *like* dogs," I protested when she appeared at my bed with a bowl of stewed mutt and herbs.

"You want to get better or not?"

I had to eat the stew several times, my malaria didn't go away, and in the bathroom one afternoon a worm wriggled partway out of me, dangling there. I shrieked and shrieked and Ah Sam came and helped me get it out. It was about eight inches long. I was given herbal pills and it took over a week to evacuate all the worms—seven in total.

"No wonder she's only forty-four pounds," my godfather said.

Years after this, a California doctor found a calcified tubercular spot on an X-ray of my left lung. But at the time, everyone thought my lungs had been weakened by malaria, and on random nights I would be wrenched awake by coughing fits—the worst of all my symptoms because they made me aware of a terrible secret within my own family.

With De-Di trying to establish himself in business and gone for days and nights at a time, my godfather Luther Chang was the most prominent man in my life. He came from an important family in Jiangxi. His sister had married T.V. Soong, the Nationalist government's Finance Minister, later the Minister of Foreign Affairs. T.V. Soong's sister had married Chiang Kai-shek. So my godfather was the brother-in-law of the brother-in-law of the President of the Republic. *One can hardly be more important than that!* I used to think. Physically, he was almost the opposite of my father: imposingly tall, formal in his bearing, aristocratic, patriarchal—a man whose every gesture expressed confidence, an inborn sense of his own authority. De-Di had a softer posture, was more loose-jointed, and looking back I like to think there was humility in the way he carried himself, a kind of humble expansiveness that reflected his desire to help the less fortunate.

Luther and my father had been fraternity brothers at Nanjing University. They had stayed in regular contact after my father, following the path of upper-class Chinese who pursued advanced degrees overseas, left for graduate school in the United States. Having earned an M.S. in Agriculture from Cornell, my father was working toward his Ph.D. when he married my mother, who likewise came from a well-to-do family and was getting her master's—at Occidental College in Los Angeles. In 1930, my parents returned to China. My father introduced his wife to his best friend and worked as Deputy Director for Guangdong's Agricultural Department until life and livelihood turned makeshift because of war.

I woke up coughing in the middle of the night, unable to breathe. No one checked on me—and wouldn't, unless I managed to cry out. I wheezed and gasped, being strangled by my own body, and just when I thought I'd suffocate in an air-filled room, the fit subsided.

I lay for some time, unable to get back to sleep.

I heard my mother call for my godfather and the whisper of his slippers as he walked to my parents' room. Gentle voices. The creak of bed boards.

I felt another bout of coughing coming on. Afraid my mother and godfather would discover I was awake, I grabbed my pillow—the one almost stolen by the Guangxi bandits—and put it over my face. The coughing fit passed, but I kept the pillow where it was, listening for my godfather's slippers shuffling back to the den. Nothing. I grew confused, my limbs went numb, and the next morning I woke up with the pillow still on my face, but wet. When it was time for Ah Sam to ready my clothes for school, I couldn't get out of bed.

"I'm too sick," I told her.

My mother came into the room and felt my forehead. "You don't have a fever," she said doubtfully.

But seeing my sweat-dampened hair and pajamas, she agreed I should stay home, and ever since then, for the past fifty-five years, I've slept with that pillow on my chest, one end of it covering my mouth but not my nose.

If Luther Chang was so well-connected, why did he live with us in a borrowed flat?

I know a few basic facts: that he had previously been married to the daughter of the Chinese Ambassador to France, and when their marriage had become particularly strained, the daughter wanted to move to France to be with her parents. Luther had no interest in leaving China and so they divorced.

But what do such facts tell me? Perhaps an old family rumor reveals more...

In Hong Kong, when I was three or four years old and Luther was already living with us, my mother announced that she no longer wanted to be married.

"Okay," my father allegedly said, "but the children stay with me."

Did my father know what was going on between his wife and fraternity brother, in which case what I called a "terrible secret" was hardly a secret at all?

While I wait for answers that will never come, the leaves on the birch trees outside my window are living and dying.

On days I wasn't sick and the weather permitted, I liked to go up to the roof garden. My mother refused to let me play in the street with other girls, fearing I'd be kidnapped and sold as a child bride or prostitute. Young girls *were* being kidnapped—Ah Sam chaperoned me to and from school on the days I attended—but I knew my mother was making excuses. All of those children being together offered a kind of protection, didn't it?

"If everyone starts screaming..." I said.

The truth was, she didn't approve of girls playing in the streets. "Don't be a tomboy," she lectured. "Nobody will want to marry you."

Would anyone ever want to marry me? I was so frail and skinny that when I wore a dress I looked more like a clothes hanger than a person, and my skin was yellow from taking quinine.

Bedridden as I too often was, not allowed to play with other girls outside, I was drawn to the open space of the roof. I spent hours there by myself. And although looking down at the streets could sting me with a keener sense of my loneliness, I usually felt a heady rush, as if I were amid all that activity: a knife sharpener with a single basket strapped to his back offering his services; a man with a one-wheeled cart selling rice flour cakes; peddlers with pushcarts towing their wares on bikes or plying their trade on foot and carrying bamboo poles across their shoulders, baskets hanging from each end filled with melon seeds, reed horns, cloth, rice, thread, fans, charcoal, pomegranate blossoms. Near the corner, a huddle of boys might be playing marbles while across the road girls amused themselves with jacks, tic-tac-toe, and their version of *jianzi*, which they called "sparrow." The sparrow was made of wadded-up newspaper and glue and bird feathers and twine. Girls competed to keep it in the air by kicking it, like juggling a soccer ball.

Summers, I'd turn my gaze skyward, watching the kites being flown by kids on nearby roof terraces.

"That's an activity for boys," my mother said when I told her I wanted to learn how to fly kites. "Why don't you have tea parties instead?"

It's true that very few girls flew kites, but I didn't care, and the next time my father was home for a couple of days, I convinced him to teach me. But it was my brother who showed me how to securely keep a kite flying above our neighborhood. Bentham was seven years my senior, and because he was at boarding school most of the year, I rarely saw him. In many ways, I was growing up as an only child in Canton. Nonetheless, from him I learned how to carefully break a glass bottle into small pieces, wrap them in cloth so as not to cut myself, and use another bottle to grind them into glass powder. I then mixed the powder with glue, coated the kite string with the paste, and laid it on the terrace to dry. Once it was dry, I rolled it onto a spool. Why? With tens of kites in the air, if one of them crashed into mine, whichever had the sharpest thread would survive. Accidental crossings happened regularly, but there were also boys who picked fights to see who had the "sharpest" string, the toughest kite.

Occasionally, I would leave my kite flying, go downstairs and rush through my dinner—Maa-Mi scoffing about how my tomboyish ways were ruining my future prospects—then hurry to the roof again to see if it was still there. It almost always was, and despite my mother, I gained confidence and self-esteem knowing that my kite was well-made and its string sharp.

My confidence and self-esteem: they weren't nurtured in school, where I was at the bottom of my class on account of missing so many lessons, and where a bully named Shuet Ching made me follow her home every lunch hour, lugging her books. I used to wish for kidnappers while I trudged along behind her. Couldn't one dart out from between the buildings and snatch my tormentor forever away? They didn't have to hurt Shuet Ching or sell her into slavery, just keep her far from my life. She made me wait outside her flat while she ate, then follow her back to school with her books, both of which I did because otherwise she threatened to get everyone in class to hate me. I believed she had such power: the few times I refused to carry her books, I was invisible to the other girls; when I carried them, at least a few classmates would sometimes talk to me.

My mother was never any help in the confidence and self-esteem department. A socialite before the wars, she wanted a daughter who was soft-spoken, always perfectly groomed, well-mannered, submissive—a daughter more like her, who made the most of her looks and was extroverted and (in public at least) light-hearted. It's curious that when she had locked me out of the flat and told me I was no longer her daughter, I'd wept and pleaded to be forgiven for something I hadn't done—curious because even at that young age, I didn't like her. But I suppose, not liking your mother, one still needs to feel her love. At six, seven, eight years old I didn't have any idea what I wanted to be when I grew up, but I knew that I hated spending all of my free time worrying about clothes and makeup and gossip, the way my mother did. She took special trips to unsafe Hong Kong to buy outfits and accessories that she forced me to wear: ruffled collar blouses, bobby socks, printed skirts and dresses, hair ribbons, and belts and shoes from Czechoslovakia.

"No other kids dress like this," I complained.

"They must be poor."

A funny thing to say, with us in Auntie Fong's flat and my father struggling to set himself up in business. But we were living an upper-middle class existence and it didn't occur to me to question her. Instead, I prayed:

"Dear God, grant me poverty so that I won't have to wear fancy imported clothes and play Maa-Mi's cute little pride and joy."

I always wanted Steve to do things my way and got upset when he didn't. I wonder if that's why he had to leave—so that I could have my way and not spend my energy trying to change him (generally, he was a considerate man). Yes, I can now be right all the time, have the best solutions for everything, and no one will argue with me! Yet I'm unhappy.

If Steve were alive, would I let him do whatever he wished? During a crisis people often promise to change for the better, hoping this will put the crisis behind them. After he was first diagnosed, I vowed: *Please God, allow him to get well and I will treat him differently, more lovingly.* It was a lie. Or if not a lie, then a naïve pledge to do the un-doable. Had Steve survived his cancer, I'm sure I would have changed for a few months at most and then reverted to my old self. But losing my husband, I lost my old self too. There's no possibility of its return, and never again will I have the pleasure of being dissatisfied with Steve, failing to get him to do things my way.

Role models? I didn't know the term when I was young, and as much as I would like to believe I invented myself, I would say, yes, I had two, one more important than the other. There was Po-Po, my step-grandmother on my father's side, who had made me eat dog stew. She lived on the eastern outskirts of Canton, raised chickens and grew vegetables, and visited every two or three weeks, bringing fresh meat and produce. She was a devout Christian and often told me stories from the Bible, teaching me about kindness, generosity, compassion, courage, love. The story of the good Samaritan, of empathy with action, made a big impression on me—maybe because, rightly or wrongly, I felt that no one had much empathy for me.

And Jesus answering said, A certain man went down from Jerusalem to Jericho, and fell among thieves, which stripped him of his raiment, and wounded him, and departed, leaving him half dead. And by chance there came down a certain priest that way: and when he saw him, he passed by on the other side. And likewise a Levite, when he was at the place, came and looked on him, and passed by on the other side. But a certain Samaritan came where he was: and when he saw him, he had compassion on him. And went to him, and bound up his wounds, and brought him to an inn, and took care of him.

This story of one stranger rescuing another from pain and hardship—how could I have known it then?—laid the groundwork for my eventual career choice. For that I owe Po-Po my thanks and love. But she was old-fashioned and favored Bentham, the family heir. On Chinese New Year, she always gave him more money in his *lai see*—many times more. The money symbolized her wish for our good fortune in the coming year. My red envelopes always looked the same as my brother's—red for good luck, joy, vitality, long life—but one holiday I was so angry with what little she'd given me compared to him that I tore up the crisp new bill and threw it in the trash. Not in front of her, though, because I didn't want to show disrespect.

My other early role model was Auntie Amy, my father's second oldest sister, who worked as a pathologist in Peking and used to stay with us for a week during the summer. If I wasn't sick in bed, she took me to Hollywood movies like *Gone with the Wind* and *A Song to Remember* and bought me American chocolates. On sick days, if I threw a tantrum—refusing to swallow castor oil, risking a beating—Auntie Amy would take the spoon and bottle from my mother and ask her to leave us alone. Sitting at my bedside, she'd listen to my complaints as I imagined she would to an adult friend.

"How scary and frustrating it must be for you to be unwell," I remember her saying. "How it must seem like you'll never get better. I'd be upset, too, in your situation."

She described new methods to treat malaria, ensuring me that I would indeed get well. Never did she raise her voice or a hand to me, and I let her spoon-feed me castor oil.

With her intelligence and self-assurance, her interest in more than just fashion or what so-and-so had said or done to whomever, I wanted both to be like Auntie Amy *and* for her to be my mother.

"So many books," she once said, looking at a little pile next to my bed. "Have you read all of these?"

In those years, books were my only steady company, my friends.

"I get them from the library," I said.

"What's your favorite?"

It was hard to choose but I told her about the story in *The Arabian*

Nights that I read in translation over and over, the one about the Sultan of India and his three sons, Prince Hussein, Prince Ali, and Prince Ahmed. All three of them wanted to marry their beautiful cousin, Princess Nur al-Nihar, and so each went off and searched the world for a precious item to prove himself worthy of her. I was the princess, of course. And as in the story, I too would be brought back to health by a magic apple, like the one Prince Ahmed found, a single sniff of which would cure me of all malady and disease. Healthy, I would fly off on Prince Hussein's magic carpet.

"With or without the prince," I said.

Auntie Amy, who wasn't married, laughed. "I agree! Why should men have all the fun traveling the world on extraordinary tapestries that take them wherever they want? You know what?" She leaned toward me as if confiding a secret. "I think you're going to travel great distances, see beautiful landscapes, and meet fascinating people in your life. A remarkable girl like you will do great things."

Her words filled me with pride and hope. Yes, I thought, prince or no prince, I would find a magic carpet and ride it far, far from my sickroom, from the bully Shuet Ching and the kids who ignored me at school, and from my mother.

"Maa-Mi's in the hospital," my father said.

I had just come home from school and found him there, unexpectedly.

"She'll be back tomorrow. You don't need to go and visit."

He didn't say what was wrong with her, and strange as it might seem, I didn't ask. I don't remember being worried, but then he didn't seem worried or upset, so why should I have been? I simply accepted what he told me. Besides, it meant an afternoon without any threat of the rattan duster.

The next day, my mother returned to the flat as if from a shopping excursion. Nothing was said about where she had spent the night, but a week later I overheard Ah Sam and another maid talking in the kitchen about how she'd had an abortion.

To no one's surprise but my own, a magic apple didn't cure me. At Auntie Amy's urging, my mother brought me to a Western doctor, and I started going to him once a week for a shot of chloroquine. My father and Luther had by now established a business importing tractors, hydraulic systems, and self-propelled combines from the US, which they rented to farmers, and De-Di used to talk excitedly during meals—not of the money the Gold Mount Import Company was making, but of how he and my godfather were helping farmers modernize their practices to achieve greater productivity and improve their lives. Luther, who I think had used his government contacts to raise the capital needed to start the business, would smile patiently at this enthusiasm. My father, he well knew, had named his only son after the British utilitarian philosopher Jeremy Bentham, who'd called for providing as much happiness, comfort, and security to the maximum number of people while harming the fewest as little as possible—hardly a philosophy embraced by many CEOs. And Luther was more of a CEO-type than my father— shrewd, smooth, and happy to help others so long as it was profitable to him. He was the Gold Mount Import's "office man," while my father—I finally learned why he was always absent—traveled to villages to promote the company's equipment and educate farmers on how their families would benefit from using it.

Life was starting to improve in the summer of 1947. The success of my father's business meant we could move into our own flat. And the chloroquine shots were helping: before the close of the year my invalid days would be over, my malaria gone. But it wasn't just my family's prospects that were on the rise, it was the whole country's. Chiang Kai-shek boasted of a full economic recovery and would soon print new money called Gold Dollar Bills. Yet when is improvement ever straightforward? The Communists, calling themselves the People's Liberation Army, picked up the weapons left by the Japanese and resumed their civil war against the Nationalist government, the Kuomintang, determined to liberate China from poverty and imperialism.

2

MAYBE I SHOULD PUSH MYSELF toward a nervous breakdown? I worked with people suffering from depression for over twenty years. Often, I advised them to let go of themselves, to stop clinging to whatever behavior they felt was necessary to survive. In surrender, I told them, things might not be as terrible as they supposed. Okay, such surrender might be different than a breakdown, but why shouldn't I court the worst, neglect the responsibilities of daily life and succumb wholly to my grief over Steve? Certainly, I don't feel like the efficient, practical woman my daughters and friends believe me to be. Why maintain the façade when I want to scream, smash, kick, destroy—and in the midst of all that, to be nourished, coddled?

This week I have not freaked out, but it's only Wednesday.

From Auntie Fong's apartment we moved into a war-ravaged building on West Bank Road, one of the busiest streets in Canton.

My father's company rented the third and fourth floors, renovating the third floor into offices and a showroom, the fourth into our residence. Our windows overlooked the Pearl River waterfront, where freighters and passenger liners from Hong Kong and Singapore docked hourly, and boat people with their sampans paddled alongside the steamers before landing and unloading their goods. The building had an elevator that didn't work most of the time, but I preferred taking the stairs anyway. I was getting stronger and more energetic by the day and spent many afternoons learning how to ride a bicycle, which I had wanted to do for years. I was under five feet tall, weighed fifty-five pounds, and had to learn on a man's bike in the showroom. The bike belonged to Ah Sing, who worked in the office. I couldn't reach the pedals from the seat, so he suggested I crouch within the frame and lean my body out one side of it while I pedaled. As I rode up and back, past gleaming equipment from America and under the amused eyes of the employees, I felt a new sense of freedom, and if it weren't for Shuet Ching, I would have been impatient for summer's end and the start of school—not because I wanted to study, but because I thought, no longer weak and sickly, I would at last make friends.

My mother was a graduate of Ginling, a Christian college in Nanjing and the first institution to grant American Bachelor of Arts degrees to women in China. At the time of her matriculation, Ginling was a sister school of Smith College in Northampton, Massachusetts. Most classes were taught in English, the girls who attended all from well-to-do, high-ranking families.

With our move to West Bank Road, my mother resumed her

pre-war socialite activities as president of her Alumnae Association. Frequently, I would tramp upstairs after practicing on Ah Sing's bike and find her hosting luncheons and ice cream parties. In addition to the Gold Mount Import Company—and because tractors and frozen treats just go together!—my father and Luther had started a retail ice cream business offering unusual flavors like black sesame. My mother both promoted and boasted of this business by having tastings, and in the company of the younger Ginling alum, she was open, lively, helpful, accommodating, full of patient advice, everything she wasn't with me. But as soon as her guests left, she would inevitably start scolding me for some new grease stain on a dress I hated wearing, or for fresh scuffs on my imported shoes that had scraped against bike pedals.

She intensified her efforts to turn me into the ideal daughter— the loveliest and most feminine, the best dressed and groomed. I was sent to "finishing" school, where I was taught to walk (I'd been doing it wrong), to engage in small talk using a pleasing voice, and to smile without showing teeth. I attended dance classes that were supposed to add grace to my every movement, and I took weekly piano lessons. I suffered through all of this, my mother informed me, in order to impress the Ginling ladies when they gathered in our flat—by walking gracefully to the baby grand and smiling demurely before I announced the title of an étude in a mellifluous voice, then dazzled with my musical skills. But guess what? We didn't have a piano!

Was my mother a bad person? I no longer think so. She had found herself stuck with the wrong husband, juggling unmet needs. Her life wasn't as good as it had been before the wars, before her marriage. Selfishness and self-pity amid an existence more fortunate than most—these aren't adequate excuses for less than ideal parenting, but people do what they do. It doesn't necessarily make them bad. I'm sure my mother was as frustrated with me as I was with her. Still, to this day there remains an unloved—for so I believed myself to be—little child inside me.

I acted out against my mother the only way I knew how, by being malicious to the maids. We had three during this time—a cook, Ah Sam, and Mo So, who was De-Di's cousin's daughter-in-law. Widowed at twenty-seven, with two young boys to raise and having no practical skills, she had been taken in by my parents.

One morning, Ah Sam brought me my clothes for the day—washed, starched, ironed.

"You have to dress me while I lie here or I won't get up," I commanded from bed.

I remained limp as she struggled to get me into my outfit, which by the end was wrinkled.

"This is unacceptable," I said. "I can't go out looking like dirty laundry."

I lay as limply as ever and Ah Sam worked hard to undress me. She ironed the clothes again—heating charcoal to put in the appliance and running it over my freshly dampened outfit. I don't know how many times I made her do this, but I remember that I felt no guilt or sympathy or compassion for her or the other maids, whom I similarly tormented.

When I was older and no longer a brat, Ah Sam admitted that she often used to cry because she didn't know what to do with me; if she had told my mother about my bad behavior, she said, I would have been beaten with the duster.

Yesterday, my younger daughter asked if I was really considering suicide.

"I'm just thinking about it," I said.

I am sorry for my behavior—she's lost her father—but can't find a way out. The problem is, I have no experience killing myself. What if I don't do a good job? How could I hold my head up in the neighborhood, with everyone knowing that I had tried to take my own life? Attempting suicide is cowardly; successful commission of it is a task well done.

"You have to allow yourself time, Mom," my daughter urged. "Be patient."

Patients. I left behind so many when I retired. I cared about all of them, whatever their problems or backgrounds. I passed up many promotions and career opportunities to avoid becoming an administrator; I preferred direct clinical experience.

I needed to be needed, I realize.

Yes, I miss my patients—partly for selfish reasons. My relationship with them inspired me, enriched my life with a purpose. I might have been their therapist and counselor, but now they counsel me by their example: however much they suffered, they had the courage and strength to go on living.

Before the start of fifth grade I decided that the best way to escape Shuet Ching would be to transfer to a different class. I told no adult of the lunch hours she had made me carry her books, or of her threats to make sure I was friendless. Instead, I let Auntie Fong know that a certain Mrs. Ling was considered the best teacher at school, and with the help of family connections, I started the academic year as a new pupil in her class. I was two years younger than the rest of the students, but because Shuet Ching wasn't among them, I didn't feel intimidated.

The desks were arranged in pairs, with a divider between them to help us focus on our work. My first day, throughout the lesson, I kept hearing weird scraping sounds on the divider. Finally, a hole popped open and a finger appeared, waving.

"Knock, knock. Anyone home?"

My deskmate's name was Chan Pei. We started passing notes back and forth, giggling about the teacher and other kids. As the weeks went on, our friendship grew and we hardly paid attention to our assignments, too busy goofing off, whispering through the hole in the divider, and carving pictures into our desks. To my surprise, without making any effort, I was no longer at the bottom of the class but routinely among the top five students. How could this be? It's true, I was attending school more regularly than in previous years, but also, for the first time since our arrival in Canton, I wasn't lonely and I think that helped make me more open and receptive.

During recess, I would follow Chan Pei down slides and up the fireman's pole as far as I could manage, and I imitated her kicking style in Sparrow—enjoying games as an eight-year-old that kids who hadn't been stricken with malaria first played when they were four or five. Chan Pei wore overalls; I wanted to wear the same (of course my mother kept me in dresses). Chan Pei was left-handed, and although Mrs. Ling forced her to use her right hand in class, I secretly practiced writing with my left hand. We walked to and from school together every day, chaperoned by Ah Sing.

"The smugglers were out again last night," she would sometimes say.

She lived in a three-story tower on a wharf at the end of West Bank Road and liked to report on her night-time sightings—guards being bribed, shadowy figures throwing their contraband over the security fence to other shadowy figures. Her excited way of telling stories was infectious, but I had nothing as darkly appealing as smuggling and bribery to offer.

"I used to have the strongest kite in the neighborhood," I said, describing how my sharp string sent lots of boys' kites sailing off into the clouds never to be seen again. I explained that I missed those mid-sky tussles, but our new building's upper floors were bombed-out, the roof terrace too treacherous with broken concrete for me to safely go up there to fly my kite. Besides, being at the mouth of the delta, the wind was too strong.

"Let's do something crazy," Chan Pei whispered on our walk one morning.

"Like what?"

She put her finger to her lips: *Shhh. You'll find out*.

As soon as Ah Sing dropped us off at school, we ran away and played hooky. We went to see *Joan of Arc*, starring Ingrid Bergman, and after the movie Chan Pei got her hair cut like the main character's: short, with bangs, a sort of layered page-boy. What she did, I had to do, so I got my hair cut too.

"What have you done to yourself?" my mother cried at the sight of me.

The problem wasn't just that I'd gotten a haircut without her permission, but that I had chosen such an unfeminine style. I accepted the wrath of her rattan duster as if I were Joan of Arc— trying not to sob, to be as quiet and hard as I could.

"You're grounded!" my mother said. "Two weeks!"

That hurt more than the beating because it meant I wouldn't be able to play with Chan Pei. The most I could do was wave at her while she stood on the pier across the street from my building—me, alone again, looking out the window at the busy world.

In America, no matter how crazy you might be, if you can work, you are considered normal. One can be a functional alcoholic. One can be a functional crazy person. But if you're retired, as I am, can you still qualify as functional crazy?

I just took the cereal boxes out of the pantry, more than half a dozen—Fruity Pebbles, Honeycomb, Rice Krispies, Alpha Bits, Golden Grahams, Frosted Flakes, Shredded Wheat (original), Grape Nuts, all open and partially eaten. I poured the cereals out on the kitchen floor and walked over the whole mess, stepping firmly to crush as much of it as possible. The question now is whether or not I should track the crumbs around the house and let someone else clean it up.

In too much of the world, people don't have enough to eat, and here I am, buying cereals by the armload only to walk on them. Most of what's on the floor was what my daughters liked when they were younger, which I supposedly keep on hand for their visits. Steve and I, because of our age, were directed by doctors to the no-fun cereals—no added sugar or trans fats, little to no salt, high fiber. There is a reason the Shredded Wheat and Grape Nuts boxes were rather full.

Steve, maybe if you had eaten more fiber-rich cereal like you were supposed to, you wouldn't have gotten cancer? Should I write letters to Post, General Mills, Kellogg, etc., telling them that they're cereals crush under foot too easily? I will wait to hear from you.

Memories are like a deck of cards; they can be endlessly re-shuffled, although I'm not always sure who the dealer is.

I want to say more about my godfather.

He insisted on eating a big breakfast every morning—bacon, eggs, toast and cereal, and he demanded that I sit down with him and eat a big breakfast also because he thought I was too skinny and it was medically sound. I was somewhat afraid of him. Yes, he had protected me from my mother on occasion, but generally he was domineering, and with his suits always perfectly pressed, his hair fastidiously combed, his shoes spit-shined, I feared and admired him from below. He could be thoughtful, however, even tender. On a short trip he made to Hong Kong, he bought me a doll I had longed for during my sick years—soft rubber and mohair, blue eyes, moveable limbs. I named her Yung-Yung.

Luther Chang: more than once I arrived home from school earlier than usual and saw him kissing my mother. Only Yung-Yung knew that I knew.

By the middle of 1948, inflation was out of control. Chiang Kai-shek, eager for the full economic recovery he'd promised, issued his Gold Dollar Bills, but it didn't help. My tuition at the start of fifth grade cost several thousand dollars. The next semester, it cost half a million. When I entered sixth grade, my family paid three million Gold Dollar Bills stuffed into a gunny sack.

Meanwhile the Communists kept gaining ground. Chiang Kai-shek expressed confidence that with America's help, he could control the spread of communism in China. No one really thought Mao would take over. Still, my maternal grandparents, who lived in the Nanjing mansion in which my mother had grown up, were persuaded by Uncle Albert to come to Canton and move in with us. Grandpa Ho, a dentist, worked until the day he left his long-time home at the age of seventy-six. My father found a clinic on Shameen Island, where he was able to volunteer twice a week. A few rich Chinese families had homes on Shameen, but most residents were British. Chan Pei and I often played there because it was relatively safe.

Suddenly, our flat was full of family twenty-four hours a day, and not just because of my grandparents, Ngoi-Gung and Ngoi-Po. My brother contracted typhoid and came home from school for six weeks. It was the longest I had lived with Bentham since Guilin, but I can't say we bonded or got to know each other much better— even if, after he recovered, he was on a strict diet and often so hungry that he would beg me to steal crackers for him. I became acquainted with more surface area of his life—he was quiet and liked boxing and cowboy movies—but there was too much distance between us in both years and upbringing for anything deeper.

When you live in the shadow of war, you have little choice but to take it as a matter of course and go about your daily life as best you can. On a family trip to Shanghai in the summer, I met my mother's eldest brother David, a bachelor in his late thirties who worked as a lawyer for the United Nations. He had a passion for Chinese antiques and took me shopping with him, teaching me about old coins, gemstones, porcelain, and jade figurines excavated from architectural sites. No one, certainly not my father or Luther, had ever let me accompany them on their outings, no matter how trivial.

"He's odd," my mother said of Uncle David.

"Bad-tempered but extremely intelligent," said my father.

That's when I started to realize I got along with the world's so-called weirdos, its most difficult people. In subsequent years, during high school and college and my postgraduate studies, whenever classmates deemed a professor odd or stingy with A's, I inevitably did well in his or her class. It was as if I had the ability to understand individuals that didn't slot easily into society's prescribed modes of behavior. Or as if I intuited that a person could exist both within those slots and outside of them at the same time. How much my years of malaria-induced isolation had to do with this, giving me the understanding and perspective of an outsider, I don't know, although the therapist in me wants to say *everything*.

By 1949, the political situation was getting dangerous. Half-starved Nationalist soldiers roamed the streets dressed in dirty old clothes, straw sandals on their feet. There were countless numbers of them squatting in the bombed-out building next door, and I sometimes watched them eating their meals from my window. Their rations, given to them twice a day, were a small bowl of brown rice with vegetables, a little meat if they were lucky.

These are troops supported by the US? I wondered in disbelief. *How can such poorly clothed and fed soldiers win any war?*

Yes, their guns and helmets were American made, but even at ten years old I assumed that someone must have pocketed most of the money sent to equip them; the Kuomintang was notoriously corrupt. I had frequently overheard my father and Luther talking about the bribes they paid government officials in order to conduct business. Unfortunately, bribes were no longer enough. My father and Luther decided we couldn't stay in Canton. But where to go?

"Macau will be a more restful place for them," Uncle Albert suggested, referring to Ngoi-Gung and Ngoi-Po.

And so it was decided: my mother and grandparents and I would go to Macau while my father and Luther stayed in Canton to wind down the Gold Mount Import Company, which had been doing poorly along with the farmers. Bentham, who was back at school, would follow us as soon as he finished eleventh grade.

Chan Pei's family decided to leave Canton as well, planning to return to Baisha, her father's village in Taishan. The day Chan Pei and I said goodbye, I invited her for ice cream on the second floor of my building, which had been renovated to supply my father's stores. We tasted every flavor and then went to the park next to our school. The park was on the grounds of Sun Yat-sen Memorial Hospital, the first Western-style hospital in China. It had been named after the Republic's first provisional president and the leader of the Nationalist party before Chiang Kai-shek; a doctor and revolutionary who helped pioneer Western medical practices in the country. Chan Pei and I weren't thinking of Sun Yat-sen in our last hour together, but I now find it remarkable that we chose to say our formal goodbyes in a place named after him—this man whose political philosophy espoused democracy and the people's welfare, both of which were in a precarious state then.

We exchanged addresses, Chan Pei and I. We promised to write and prayed that somehow either Mao and his army would retreat or Chiang Kai-shek would reclaim the mainland so that we could soon be together again in Canton. We walked home slowly, in silence. As we approached my building, my heart started palpitating, my hands went cold, and I could feel the blood rushing like worms inside me. I thought I was going to vomit.

"Take care," Chan Pei said. "We'll meet again."

Both of us were crying. We barely looked at each other, and we didn't hug because it wasn't a Chinese habit. Chan Pei walked quickly toward the wharf. I rushed up to my flat and kicked at the front gate to be let inside.

"What's the problem?" Ah Sam asked.

I ran to the balcony without answering and looked out to where my best friend lived, hoping that amid all the activity on the street I might catch a last glimpse of her.

3

I DREAMT THAT I WOKE UP at the bottom of a trench. Gun smoke hovered in the air overhead. I had been digging with my partner during the battle, I remembered, but now I was alone. And in pain. I checked myself for wounds—had none that I could see. I called for help but was unable to hear my own voice. Managing to get to my feet, I peered out at the surrounding wasteland. Burnt trees, boot prints, no weapons or bodies. It wasn't dark but I couldn't distinguish whether it was day or night. Everything was still except for the slowly drifting gun smoke.

I wanted to climb free of the trench but didn't know if I could because of the pain throughout my body. Where would I go, anyway? What difference would it make to my existence? If I went back to sleep, I thought, I might wake to a different scene. I could try. I *was* tired. I lay down again, but as I closed my eyes in the dream, I awoke alone in my too-large bed.

Steve, I miss you with all of your strengths and weaknesses. I miss the whole of you. Also, I can't continue to lose weight.

It's ironic that Macau became something of a haven for refugees during both World War II and the Communist takeover of China. In the nineteenth century, it had been infamously associated with the "coolie" trade, its port the last thing kidnapped victims saw as they were shipped off to Cuba, Peru, and other parts of South America to labor in mines and on plantations—if they arrived anywhere at all, since like the slaves bound for America, many of them died at sea from malnutrition, disease, violence. Yet it *was* the closest we had to a haven. Macau, being a Portuguese colony, had essentially been left alone by the Japanese during the war, and the Communists had enough to do without actively challenging Portuguese authority.

The first day I arrived, I started writing to Chan Pei. Was she aware that Macau was sometimes called the Monte Carlo of the East because of its gaming business? Or that with its cobblestone streets and tree-lined riverfront, it resembled a quaint European town? I knew nothing of quaint European towns. I had read this description in a book, having done homework on my new home in order to write to Chan Pei about it. I described our cottage on Guia Hill, situated in the shadow of the Portuguese fortress, a seventeenth-century military complex with a lighthouse built on the peninsula's highest point. And I went on at length about Penha Chapel, a beautiful church erected by followers of St. Augustine, even describing the statue of Our Lady of Lourdes that faces out to sea from the courtyard, her hands clasped, her expression peaceful.

"She's praying for the protection of the sailors and tradespeople and fishermen on the ocean," I wrote, wondering why she didn't also pray for those abducted into slavery.

What I didn't tell Chan Pei, because I didn't know it then, was that despite being the majority, Chinese people in Macau were looked down upon by the Portuguese and Macanese. Mixed descendants of Portuguese and Tanka, or "boat people," the Macanese had historically been considered outcasts by native Chinese, so I guess it was their chance to make others feel as lowly as they had been made to feel. In coming years, I often thought it wouldn't hurt the statue at Penha Chapel to turn toward town once in a while and pray for the safety and well-being of those suffering discrimination right beneath her nose.

Accustomed to their mansion in Nanjing, its five acres planted with corn and vegetables and a tenderly cultivated English garden, my grandparents hadn't expected to live in such a humble cottage—even after the flat in Canton. None of us did.

"It's only temporary," my mother said.

At least Ngoi-Gung and Ngoi-Po had their own room. My brother, when he joined us at the end of his school year, slept in a single bed in my mother's room while I made camp in a hall adjacent to a storage area. I had no privacy, but my bed was next to a window and I could indulge my old habit of gazing out at the world—passing neighbors, romping dogs and basking cats, the elm tree whose shade kept the cottage relatively cool in the subtropical summer—and pretend I wasn't missing Chan Pei.

One of the maids slept practically on top of me in the storage area. The other had to put out a cot in the living room at night. These weren't the same maids from Canton. Ah Sam and Ah Chut and the cook were gone, as was Ah Sing from my father's office.

We shed people like old skin in those times.

Where would my godfather sleep when he came to live with us? I didn't ask.

My brother wasn't in Macau more than a couple of weeks before he said he wanted to finish high school in Canton.

"None of my friends are here," he complained.

None of mine either, I thought. *Or Maa-Mi's.*

But my mother was quickly establishing a small social circle that included Mrs. Wong, the busybody of Macau, whom we called #23 Aunt because she was the twenty-third child in her family; her father had several wives.

"You want to go back?" my mother said, as if trying to understand a foreign language.

Every day, the radio and newspapers updated us on the Communists—how they were taking over the country province by province, establishing the People's Republic of China. Some of us still had faith in Chiang Kai-shek's promise that he and his forces, retreating to Taiwan, would return backed by the superior military power of the United States; Voice of America and other Nationalist government sources in Taiwan kept broadcasting reports of an imminent offensive to retake the mainland. Whether Bentham believed this or he was already ideologically aligned with the Communists, I can't say. But he argued that he was among thousands of political refugees in Macau on waiting lists for high schools. Who knew when or *if* he would get into one? Besides, our father was in Canton.

"It will only be temporary," he said, echoing what had become my mother's go-to phrase whenever we complained.

He left at summer's end. I didn't see him again for ten years, and then only for three weeks, after which I didn't see him again for another twenty. With the Communist "liberation" of China, I lost what little relationship with Bentham that I'd had.

It's only temporary.

Steve tended toward stopgap solutions—a way to remedy a situation quickly, to get someone off his back or summarily finish a task. He was never concerned about whether a problem was "solved" as long as it no longer plagued him at the moment.

"If you settled on a good solution to begin with, you wouldn't have to work at it a second and third time," I commented more than once, to his irritation.

"You always think you know best."

"No, I just try to solve problems so they won't have to be dealt with again and again."

But most solutions have to be reworked, don't they? Survival, after all, is a series of stopgap measures, temporary fixes. Until it isn't.

The People's Republic of China versus the Republic of China: most Americans find it confusing despite being taught to distrust if not hate communism almost from birth. But most Americans never try to understand. The Communists on the mainland are the People's Republic and the Democratic Nationalists in Taiwan represent the Republic? They assume such dynamics have nothing to do with them, so why should they care?

"Because," I say, referring to the old proverb, "the flapping of a butterfly's wings can be felt on the other side of the world."

My father was still in Canton when the Communists took over the country in October, 1949. During the previous months of turmoil, with so many others scrambling to relocate their businesses and families, he'd been unable to arrange transportation of the ice cream manufacturing equipment. Then it was too late to sell; the new government confiscated everything he and Luther owned, including the remainder of the Gold Mount Import Company's assets—its trucks, bikes, scooters, supplies, and machinery.

He arrived in Macau subdued and distracted, uncertain how to provide for us. De-Di was old-fashioned in this regard. He believed that financially supporting the family was a man's job, and he wouldn't talk to my mother about business or household finances. Not that she didn't try.

"You always have more than enough for what you need and the kids' tuition," he'd say. "Don't worry."

I was attending an all-girls Christian school by that time, as I had in Canton, and one afternoon I told him how embarrassing my first day had been—and every day since—because Maa-Mi continued to dress me in flowery skirts and ruffled blouses, with ribbons tied in my hair.

"The other kids laugh at me," I said.

He gently smiled and said, Did I know that after Bentham was born, he had hoped for a daughter?

I did not. His preference was unusual, Chinese men generally wanting as many sons as possible, but I didn't understand how this would help me.

"I'd like to wear comfortable clothes," I said. "A lot of girls wear pants or overalls and they're not tomboys."

I also complained about how strict Maa-Mi had become, requiring me to give at least a week's notice for anything I wanted to do, even see a movie. Her rigidity prevented me from making any close friends because my classmates often got together spontaneously. And as far as I could tell, it had little to do with a desire for my safety; when I *was* allowed out, with no Ah Sing or anyone else to chaperone me, I walked the streets alone.

"I'll talk to her," he promised.

A few mornings later, while I was still in bed, one of the new maids brought in my outfit for the day: a pair of overalls and a simple white shirt. From then on, I was allowed to wear comfortable clothes a couple of times a week, but I didn't have a chance to thank my father; he had already left to join Luther in Hong Kong and explore new business opportunities.

What can you tell about a person from their economy?

Steve always bought good quality clothes—Cable Car, Bullocks and Jones, Brooks Brothers. But only when they were on sale and even if he didn't particularly like them. As a result, his wardrobe was consistently out of style, his slacks and button-downs and sport coats in odd colors.

"You buy nice things but hardly wear them," I said, "so although you buy them on sale, you don't get much for your money."

Why did I feel the need to comment on this harmless little quirk?

Why couldn't I find it adorably amusing? Or remind myself that Steve had come to this country when he was seven, after his father, a veteran of World War II, was finally allowed to send for his wife and son; and that he had grown up on the cusp of poverty, with a single pair of jeans and no real shoes until the big outing of his young life—to Florsheim?

It does no good, chastising myself for not having appreciated Steve every second when he was alive, for not being acutely aware of the love we had for each other, instead of rearing into petty annoyance because he wasn't me and didn't do as I would managing the smallest details of our day-to-day.

It does no good, and yet...

Feeling guilty, I open closets and drawers full of barely used clothes, making no effort to part with any of them.

Enjoying more latitude with my wardrobe, I wrote to Uncle David, the U.N. lawyer, and asked if he wouldn't mind sending me a pair of American jeans. He didn't know how skinny I was, and I received a pair of Levi's several sizes too large. No tailor would alter them because of their metal tabs. I asked Ah Ying, the maid who did everything but cook, to repeatedly wash them, but they didn't shrink enough to fit. Unable to wear the jeans to school, wide and baggy as they were, I wore them at home constantly—or nearly. My mother made me change out of them whenever she had guests.

Why did I treasure my Levi's? Because they came from America— that rich land I dreamed of one day flying to on a magic carpet, where my parents and many of my uncles and aunts had received postgraduate degrees, and where a number of them, because of war, had stayed and made prosperous lives for themselves. But my jeans did more than just represent freedom and possibility; they provided them. I could literally tumble around, physically do whatever I had a mind to do, no longer constricted by the expensive dresses I'd been forced to wear for so long, with my mother always warning me to be careful and not get them dirty.

Considering it now, my mother's blind spot strikes me as odd. She wasn't far removed from the years when it had been a wide-spread custom for women to have their feet bound—a practice that started with the upper classes. Bound feet were a status symbol, declaring that you were one to be waited upon and lived a life of leisure. Girls usually went through the initial ritual between five and eight years old. An elder woman of the family or a professional foot-binder would first offer prayers to the Tiny-Footed Maiden Goddess and Guanyin before getting to work, leaving the young girl's big toes alone while bending the eight smaller ones down toward her soles, then tightly wrapping each foot with long strips of cloth. Until the girl reached her teens, the bindings would be removed once a month to treat infections, ulcerations, and to amputate any gangrenous toes. The history books say that this practice kept a girl's feet from growing and that small feet were considered beautiful. I'm no historian but I can tell you—it's an ugly sight, those gnarled toes crushed down against a misshapen knob of an arch.

Foot-binding eventually spread to the villages, the lower classes. Maybe people were being aspirational, trying to improve a daughter's social prospects, or maybe they were simply emulating their alleged superiors. But there is no doubt that the practice rendered rural women tractable, limiting their mobility so much that even walking was a chore. It effectively kept them at their looms and other domestic work, dependent on men.

All of which my mother knew. She had gone to Occidental to get her master's in Physical Education, intending, before she married, to bring the love of exercise and physical self-determination to Chinese women. Yet she didn't seem to understand what my Levi's gave to me.

Some blind spots are willful, others less so. Would I like my daughters to point out mine?

In many families, there are favorite sons and daughters. My mother was nobody's favorite. Auntie Lily, who had received a master's degree in music composition from USC, was Ngoi-Po's favorite daughter; Auntie Doris, who had studied social work at Columbia in New York City and came to live nearby in Macau after the Communist takeover, was Ngoi-Gung's. Uncle Guy, a dentist and professor in Los Angeles, was Ngoi-Gung's favorite son; Uncle David was Ngoi-Po's.

Whenever my mother entertained Mrs. Wong and other friends at the cottage, Ngoi-Po would go on and on about Auntie Lily—how she'd married an entrepreneur, how she and her husband had been among the first, if not the first, Chinese to buy property in Beverly Hills. She related these things as if to highlight my mother's failings by comparison—my mother, who never wavered from the role of gracious host while her friends were there, or dutiful daughter when they weren't.

"Why don't you go outside and sit under the elm tree?" she might suggest to Ngoi-Gung.

"What for?" he'd scoff.

But if Auntie Doris dropped by and suggested he sit under the elm tree to enjoy a bit of fresh air, off he'd go.

Did my mother hope that by taking care of her parents, she might rise in their esteem? Why didn't they live with Doris, one of their favorites, instead of stewing in a cottage that was too small to house their complaints, with a daughter whose efforts to please them and make them comfortable they dismissed?

My mother had a rival for her parents' least favorite: her youngest brother Ernest, who contracted tuberculosis as a teenager and intermittently suffered from it the rest of his life. Before I was born, he had killed a man in a hunting accident, and Ngoi-Gung had used his influence as a prominent Nanjing citizen to keep him from prison or worse. He was quiet and mild-mannered, but not—I used to overhear my parents say—very bright or blessed with good luck.

Struggling to make a living in Shanghai, he came to Macau, having been given a job by Uncle Albert, his entrepreneurial brother-in-law who lived in Beverly Hills. Unassuming and feckless: it's no wonder Ngoi-Gung didn't favor Ernest; he didn't like to recognize such characteristics in a son.

"Greet him and then hurry off," my mother would say whenever he visited the cottage, fearing I would catch TB.

She and my father, Ngoi-Gung and Ngoi-Po—they all kept their distance from him, and the cottage was unfailingly aired out after he left.

"Why is he always coming here for help with that girl?" Ngoi-Po complained, referring to Uncle Ernest's fiancée, a woman coincidentally named Lily, who everyone in my family said was spoiled and bad-tempered.

She did seem so. She frequently stormed into the cottage, ranting and raving—about nothing and everything. Uncle Ernest's failings. The boredom of being in Macau. Street noises. She and my uncle eventually got married and moved to Hong Kong. Her ranting and raving didn't stop. She demanded a divorce, then killed herself by jumping off a high-rise before it was finalized.

None of us had understood: Lily hadn't been spoiled and bad-tempered but mentally unstable—bipolar.

Meek, indecisive, plagued by bad karma. Might we have as easily described Uncle Ernest as gentle, sensitive, and good natured, even perhaps wracked by guilt over having accidentally killed a man?

I remember we were out to dinner at a restaurant—me, my mother, and grandparents. Ngoi-Gung was criticizing the food and service, and I excused myself to go to the bathroom, where I discovered brown spots on my underwear. I waited until we got home to show my mother.

"It's started," she said.

About a year before, noticing that my breasts were developing, she had talked to me about menstruation. There would come a time when I'd bleed monthly, she had said, explaining what a girl did to keep herself neat and tidy. I hadn't fully understood her, but I hadn't liked what I heard.

"It happens to all girls at a certain age, usually between eleven and fourteen."

"I'm only ten."

"There's no harm in talking about it."

In Macau, after looking at my underwear, she gave me a Kotex belt and some pads and showed me how to use them—one of the few practical things she ever taught me. For the next while, the old constriction was back, no matter whether I was dressed in overalls or jeans; the Kotex belt and pad, the cramps, they limited my physical freedom.

"I hate this," I told my mother. "If I have to keep doing it, I'd rather die."

"Don't be ridiculous."

"Does this happen to tomboys?"

She didn't like that and stomped off—to get the rattan duster, I thought. But no.

Taking menstruation as a sign that I was growing up, my mother decided to give me a weekly allowance.

"It's for Kotex, snacks at school, and going to the movies."

It wasn't customary in China for a child to be given an allowance, especially a girl. Whenever any of my classmates needed money, they just asked their parents for it.

Here, then, was another practical thing my mother taught me, although indirectly because I had to figure it out on my own: how to manage money, to prioritize expenditures and save what I could. This gift she was giving me, of learning to be financially independent, I eventually found out had been handed down to her from Ngoi-Po. The past, good and bad, reverberates through the generations, no matter how you might try to ignore it or convince yourself otherwise.

In a time when China was divided among many kingdoms, war and loss of territory forced Grandpa Ho's ancestors south, to Fujian province. The locals didn't accept them, branding them Hakka—"guest people"—and so they lived in the mountains as a self-contained community, erecting castle-like fortifications called round houses or *tulou*. Typically donut-shaped, these were large, three-story structures complete with turrets and battlements that accommodated up to seventy families, with central open courtyards where residents worshipped, did their laundry, raised chickens, and grew produce. But the mountain soil was stingy, the neighbors remained unfriendly if not always hostile, and over the centuries some Hakka moved further south to Guangdong.

In the late 1800s, my great-grandfather's poor, young family were precariously settled outside Kowloon. Ngoi-Gung was three years old when his father, desperate for a better life, signed a five-year contract to work on a sugarcane plantation in Hawaii, earning three dollars a month, plus food, clothing, and a place to live. He was allowed to bring his wife and toddler son on the three-month voyage to Kona.

For upwards of ten hours a day, twenty-six days a month, spurred to productivity by whip-carrying overseers, my great-grandfather worked the land—digging, planting, fertilizing, weeding, and harvesting. Was this a better life? It hardly seems so. The family was still poor by the time Ngoi-Gung had four younger siblings and started going to school. Every day his mother sent him off with a rice ball and salted duck egg for lunch. Instead of eating the whole egg, however, he would crack the top of it and use a toothpick to eat a small bit, making sure to get some of the yolk. In this way, surviving largely on a single rice ball a day, my grandfather made one duck egg last him the whole week, and he would give the other four to his younger siblings—for whose welfare, as the eldest, he felt somewhat responsible.

In the 1890s he was old enough to attend college—and *would* have, if not for a racist law that restricted Chinese to working in the fields and in rice or sugar mills. Thankfully, there are always a few who defy the racism of their age, and Grandpa Ho was taken on as a dentist's apprentice. The law prevented him from ever getting licensed as a dentist himself, but he learned the trade well and treated his earnings like those salted duck eggs, saving enough to occasionally loan money to good friends. One such friend, Li, another Chinese immigrant, couldn't repay his debt after his business suspiciously burned down, and in lieu of payment he offered his sister Fai, who was then living in Hong Kong, as a wife. Li could do this. It was tradition; wives obeyed their husbands, but if a husband passed away, they obeyed their sons— as did any daughters. Both of Fai's parents had died when she was young, leaving family decisions to her older brother, and so instead of going to college as she intended, my grandmother traveled to Honolulu for an arranged marriage, and Li's debt was forgiven.

Not used to the climate, Ngoi-Po frequently fell ill. Although she managed to give birth twice (Auntie Lily and my mother were born on the island), after a couple of miscarriages Ngoi-Gung decided that they should return to China for her health. They landed in Nanjing, in the waning years of the Qing Dynasty, about 1907.

Before their arrival, dental care in Nanjing had been cartoonish—people yanking out rotten teeth with the help of string and doorknobs, that sort of thing. There were no licenses or permits to be had. Grandpa Ho simply started seeing patients. Years passed, his reputation reached such a degree that high-ranking government officials came to him for his expertise, and one night after hours—in the early 1930s, I believe—he received a call from Chiang Kai-shek's assistant: the President of the Republic had a toothache and wanted to see him. Ngoi-Gung, giving no thought to possibly having his head chopped off or "being disappeared" for insubordination, told the assistant that the President would have to wait until the office opened the next day, that he was welcome to the ten o'clock slot but the nine o'clock was already booked. I assume Chiang Kai-shek was satisfied with the treatment he received, since my grandfather continued to practice for more than a decade afterward.

As good at dentistry as he was, his frugality kept him from being a great businessman. Ngoi-Po handled the finances and invested his earnings in real estate, which enabled them to move into their mansion. And it was Ngoi-Po—a woman who had come of age when foot-binding was pervasive and had abided by the tradition of obeying the men in her family—who made sure her three daughters were highly educated, sending them to Ginling college and then to graduate school in America, wanting to empower them, to give them the choice of independence that she herself never had.

I admit that I find it difficult to reconcile this determined, independent-minded, business-savvy woman with the one I knew in Macau, even though she frequently encouraged me to study hard and be self-sufficient and not live a life like hers.

"If I'd only had an education," she would say, dipping her head toward her husband, "I could have left him and had a career of my own."

But then, too many times she sat quietly and apologetically through his incessant scolding—of the maids, and of my mother who could do nothing right. Ngoi-Gung's temper had been bad all his life, but it became worse as his glaucoma progressed, and when things finally came to a violent head, it wasn't independence-minded Ngoi-Po or my mother who stood up to him.

Fuck. Shit. Crap. Damn. I have been using four-letter words a lot.

This afternoon, I was invited to dinner at our former neighbors'—Steve, you remember Deb and Matt?—and thinking it might force me to eat a full meal, that I wouldn't just sit and watch my hosts gorge while I childishly pushed vegetables around on my plate, I said, "Why the fuck not? That'd be fuckingly fabulous."

Deb—still the archetype of a beautiful blonde white American woman—was half-drunk when I got to her home, and without going into details she immediately confided that her marriage was in trouble. By dinner she was completely drunk and couldn't keep her eyes open. Matt—as handsome as ever—pretended not to notice and filled me in on neighborhood happenings: Robert and Linda moved to New York; Laura is involved with a man who totally controls her; Nancy and Michael are divorced; Doug has grown more eccentric and become something of a shut-in.

Steve, I'd hoped that seeing our old neighbors might bring back happy memories of when we first retired and moved to Alameda and everything had seemed fuckingly fabulous. But I grew tired. I didn't want to hear about anyone else's problems, what changes were wrought by the relentless passage of time. I did eat half of my baked salmon and a few string beans, but I left when dessert was offered.

I am now at home. It's only eight-thirty and a long night looms. I look at my calendar. How the fuck am I to survive all the empty days ahead of me?

The political atmosphere in Macau? I remember it as largely pro-Communist. There was always some form of propaganda going on—plays, movies, exhibits that celebrated communism's promise of a poverty-free society or presented regional folk dances as treasures of Chinese culture. I didn't attend as many Communist functions as most of my classmates, unable to summon hatred for a capitalism that had produced my Levi's. And when I did attend, it was only to be with my closest friend at the time—Tsang Shuet King, a pretty, slightly chubby girl.

Like #23 Aunt, Shuet King's father had three wives. The first, whom she addressed as Mother, hadn't birthed any sons, so her husband had had "the right" to take another. Shuet King's actual mother, whom she called Auntie, gave birth to two sons, but when it was doubted that she'd produce more children because of her age, Shuet King's father, wanting more sons, had married a third time.

I had always looked down on concubine culture, a prejudice I learned from my Westernized family. But after I met Shuet King, well...she was quick to smile—genuinely, it seemed to me—and I rarely did. So who could say for sure that concubine culture was worse than having affairs with your husband's best friend? Worse than letting your brother dictate whom you married, or spending your entire adult life with an incompatible spouse because, for your generation and social status, divorce was socially taboo?

Of course, I have no idea how Shuet King's three mothers felt about their lives.

Fleeing the Communists, my role model aunt had left her pathologist job in Peking and come to live with us, sleeping on the single bed in my mother's room.

"Can you make me something like this?" I asked Shuet King, showing her one of Auntie Amy's chest binders—a tight-fitting band she wore to flatten her breasts because, in her thirties, still unmarried and consequently considered an "old maid," she wasn't supposed to draw attention to herself as a sexual creature.

"Yes, I think so," Shuet King said, too modest to ask why I wanted a chest binder.

Good at sewing, she made a few of them for me. Every morning, I left the cottage dressed in outfits chosen by my mother, but as soon as I got to school, I hurried to the bathroom and changed out of my bra, flattening my breasts. I did feel awkward in my body at that time, and I was confused and excited by my first sexual urges, but these had little to do with my motivation; I was simply imitating Auntie Amy, and I took it so much for granted that she was above all social conventions and did as she pleased, it never occurred to me to wonder why she chose to wear chest binders in keeping with what was expected of "old maids."

Almost daily, I debated whether to tell her what I was doing. I didn't doubt her approval, but I feared it might be outweighed by an obligation she felt to inform my mother. Anyway, before I could decide, she moved out. Unable to find rewarding work in Macau, unhappy about living with bitter, complaining Grandpa Ho, she decided that she'd be better off with the Communists and returned to her old job in Peking. I continued to wear chest binders for a year—up until #23 Aunt, nosey as she was, happened to mention to my mother that she'd seen me on the street outside school and noticed that my breasts had curiously disappeared.

"Why would she say that?" my mother asked.

"I don't know."

She gave me a look. "You don't know, huh?"

Rifling through my things, she confiscated my chest binders in a rage, and not wanting to hear about my admiration for her sister-in-law, beat me with the rattan duster.

Earlier, I said that I learned how to manage money on my own, to live on a budget, and it's true, although my mother did require me to keep a log detailing how I spent my allowance. She looked over this log once in a while, checking it like a schoolmarm, but generally, because I was always able to save a little something every week, she made no comments. However, after Ngoi-Gung went blind and his temper worsened, my mother, who had no sway over her parents, tried to exert more control over me. She started criticizing me for expenditures here and there, even though I was still saving money. Also, she chastised me for being clumsy and untidy, making messes that she or Ah Ying had to clean up, and for my un-lady-like eating habits.

"Eat slowly," she would admonish. "Take smaller bites."

I was better off with malaria, I thought when particularly irked. *At least then I was mostly left alone.*

Years of illness had made me a picky eater. In Canton, my mother had accepted this as a symptom of my disease. But now that I was well, she seemed to think I should eat whatever was put in front of me—vegetables especially, as if I had to make up for the ones I hadn't eaten when I was sick. We didn't have beef often because it was expensive, but when we did, I had to finish all of my vegetables before I was allowed a single bite of it. On my secret list of reasons for wanting to fly off to America, beef was near the top. I longed to be in a place where beef was plentiful.

My brother returned to Macau after finishing high school. Excited by communism's potential, he talked to anyone who would listen, and several who wouldn't, about ridding the world of imperialism and inequity. He wanted to go to Beijing, the new capital, for college.

"Absolutely not," my mother said.

My father was briefly back from Hong Kong, preoccupied—my mother and I were unaware of this—because his new business of importing hardware to the mainland was collapsing, a result of the US's tightening restrictions on the sale of military technology and infrastructure to the People's Republic.

"He is eighteen," he said of Bentham, "old enough to decide for himself."

My mother brooded. "You can go to Beijing on one condition," she finally said. "That you promise to study medicine."

Naively, she thought Bentham would be respected as a doctor, no matter the political system he lived under. But although he kept his word, graduating from medical school in Beijing in 1954, she never forgave my father for having let her only son largely decide his own future and go to the capital in the first place.

Yes, I had a secret list of reasons for traveling to America. The example of Uncle Albert—my mother's brother-in-law, the world-class businessman and resident of Beverly Hills—had inspired me to articulate what I wanted and why. A year before the People's Republic of China was established, he'd advised Ngoi-Gung to sell his mansion in Nanjing and move his assets to Hong Kong. Whether Ngoi-Po agreed with this advice or not, I don't know, but my grandfather refused to follow it. I suppose his identity was too tied up with that large house, his local real estate holdings, his many servants—what he had to show for forty years of hard work and proof of how far he'd come as a coolie's son. All of which he had lost anyway.

Uncle Albert had business interests in Hong Kong and Southeast Asia, and every year he took time out of his schedule to visit us in Macau for a day or two. He always gave me *lai see* and asked about school.

"Study hard and get good grades," he said, "and you can come to America for your graduate education."

Ngoi-Po would inevitably ask him to tell us about how he'd bought his house in Beverly Hills.

With a knowing smile, he would begin as if narrating a Hollywood movie. "It was the late 1920s, I was working in my family's gift shop in San Diego, and I let it be known that I planned on going to college after high school."

I knew this story by heart, not only from my uncle's repeated recitations, but from my grandmother's too, since she regaled

Maa-Mi's friends with it.

"College?" Albert's uncle had scorned, telling him to go to the mirror. "Look at your face. You're yellow. They'll never accept you. You can't amount to anything with that yellow face."

But Albert was determined. He attended USC, selling insurance on the side, and graduated summa cum laude with enough money saved to start his own business. He married Auntie Lily, his import/export concern thrived, and he thought, Why not live in Beverly Hills? Well, because no one in Beverly Hills would sell to a Chinese! But Uncle Albert again refused to accept the limitations of the status quo. He enlisted the help of a Jewish friend, one of his fraternity brothers from USC, who bought a Beverly Hills property and then sold it to him.

Despite seeing him just once a year during our time in Macau, it was Albert who most instilled in me the idea that America is a land of freedom and opportunity—which, yes, while it may remain a myth for the less fortunate, is very much a reality for the Uncle Alberts of the world.

Bentham wasn't alone in his zeal for communism; lots of young people anticipated great things of Mao's government, and Chinese from around the world were returning to the mainland. It's true, however, that many of the returnees were being discriminated against elsewhere—not just in Malaysia, the Philippines, and Indonesia either. Thanks to Senator McCarthy, prominent Chinese scientists and doctors were harassed into leaving America, giving the lie to my mother's belief that doctors would always be respected. Some, then, traveled back to the mainland because they were filled with idealistic dreams; others had little choice but to hope communism would prove a kinder alternative to racism. Some of my classmates planned to follow my brother's path of going to Beijing to further their education and serve the people. My old friend Chan Pei, it turned out, would be one of them.

4

THE CRAB APPLE AND PLUM TREES ARE BLOOMING pink and our sand-stone-colored house—the color you chose, Steve—looks lovely amid the flowers and healthy green of the lawn.

This evening I took Napoleon out for a stroll, as you used to do when you still had the strength. How you spoiled him! We pass a certain lamppost, he looks up at me with eager eyes, his mouth open for a treat. We come to a specific bend along the lagoon, he expects another treat. I never refuse him, and we continue on, tracing your steps as best we can, no footprints to follow except in memory.

I remember how you struggled to walk again after each surgery—how, after your last procedure and doctors had told you the truth, you worked to get out of bed as soon as possible and take Napoleon for his neighborhood ramble. I accompanied you until you felt confident enough to go on your own, and then...well, I never shared your confidence. Did you pretend not to know that I trailed you, out of sight, in case you needed help? You always had such inner strength, and proved to be braver than I could ever be.

Worried, anxious, I became angry when you had no appetite.

"I'm trying," you said one evening. "Believe me, I want to eat the soup. Just give me a little time."

I knew you were trying. And if I was exhausted, how much more so must you have been? But I couldn't help losing my temper.

In healthier days, during an argument, you said to me, "I'm working so hard for you, to give you what you would have had."

I didn't understand: What I *would have* had? You always thought, in marrying you, that I'd married below my status—you, from the villages, a grocer's son who had lived above his family's modest shop in South Central, with fruit crates for furniture; me, born in Hong Kong to educated parents, attended to by maids, the granddaughter of Chiang Kai-shek's dentist, with one uncle in Beverly Hills and another a professor of dentistry at USC. But Steve, I never regretted my choice.

Seasons pass—fall, winter, part of autumn, almost a whole year that is unknown to you.

Principal Lee escorted a new student into my eighth-grade classroom in the middle of a lesson. It was like sunlight suddenly piercing a dark room: Chan Pei, the friend I'd left fifteen months before! I didn't get a chance to talk to her until lunch. Her father had been purged from his village by the Maoists but he'd bribed an official to let the family escape.

"You never wrote me back," I said and tried for a sad, pouty expression because I had been sending her letters every few weeks, but I was too happy to be with her again.

We resumed our old habit of going to weekly movies, although we never skipped school to see them, Shuet King frequently came with us, and the dark theaters weren't the refuge they used to be; we had to stay alert for soldiers who might move stealthily closer to flirt and touch us. I still considered Chan Pei my best friend, but after more than a year's separation, our relationship just wasn't the same. The fact that she was two years older, at a later stage of development and awakening, started to make a difference.

Girls in my middle school ranged in age from twelve to seventeen, the wars having delayed the education of many. As one of the youngest students, I felt out of place with the older kids, but Chan Pei made friends with quite a few of them. They lived in the same area of town as she did, and she walked home with them in the afternoon, Shuet King too—a pack of giggling, gossiping girls. No one lived near me on Guia Hill, and I had to walk home by myself, brooding and jealous.

Not infrequently, as I made my lonely way home, I would find myself surrounded by Macanese boys. The first time it happened I stood paralyzed with fright, unable to breathe, while they made rude, suggestive gestures and insulted me because I wasn't Macanese. I closed my eyes, expecting the worst—not that I knew what *that* was—and heard only the blood rushing through my head. When I opened my eyes again, the boys were loping off down the street. The next time I was accosted, I felt similarly afraid, but I managed to keep walking and the boys let me pass. They grew bolder after that, sometimes blocking my way and getting handsy. Once, I screamed to get them to leave me alone. This attracted the attention of nearby soldiers, but knowing *they* could be worse than the

Macanese, I ran off while they were berating the boys.

I began taking different routes home that were sometimes three times longer than they needed to be—turning a random corner if I saw two or more Macanese boys down the block, hurrying to the next corner and darting out of sight before they could catch a glimpse of which way I'd gone.

"Who are you running from?"

These were his first words to me—a tall man with a squarish, pock-marked face, a metallic sheen to his skin. Chan Pei soon after dubbed him Mechanical Man; I wasn't the only one he exposed himself to.

Who was I running from?

He didn't wait for an answer before his coat flared open, revealing his erect penis, and he started to masturbate, whistling as if engaged in a hobby like some—I apologize for the pun—woodworker. I tried to ignore him, but he followed me, urging me to stop and watch. I walked past my house, then scurried this way and that, circling back after I'd lost him to keep him from knowing where I lived.

Over and over again I had run-ins with the Macanese boys and the Mechanical Man, and meanwhile Chan Pei and her ninth-grade friends were attending Communist functions across town, growing more progressive.

In Canton, we had gone solely to Hollywood movies. We'd preferred them to the Chinese, which were invariably about war with Japan, because they often had happy endings—at least for the main characters—and they improved our English. But in Macau, Chan Pei suggested we start going to movies about revolution and lifting people out of poverty.

"Your colonial mentality is being shaped by the Capitalists," she said.

I wanted to remind her that the Communists had purged her father from his village, but I didn't, afraid I would lose her friendship. I was always fearful that love or affection, whether a friend's or parent's, would be taken from me if I truly expressed myself.

"Sorry," I murmured and kept going to Hollywood movies on my own.

"To bring back to Nanjing," Ngoi-Po said, putting a newly purchased porcelain rice bowl in her blind husband's hands and letting him feel its contours. She described the bowl's pastel-colored illustrations. "It's hand-painted with a heron and a lily."

Such moments were the only time Ngoi-Gung wasn't scolding someone. His fingers traced along the rim of the bowl, his lips trembled.

My grandparents still hoped to return to their mansion, although there was no indication that Chiang Kai-shek was going to retake the mainland. Even I knew they wouldn't see it again, that it would have been turned into multi-family housing or torn down as a symbol of colonialism. But still the charade went on—

"To bring back to Nanjing," Ngoi-Po would say, putting a rice bowl or jade sculpture or iron tea kettle into her husband's hands.

They had become nobodies in a strange land, unable to bear the thought of never returning to their home, of dying in Macau. That's war for you. It forces people to make sacrifices from which there is no healing.

Big Bird: the name I gave to the heron Steve and I met when we first moved from McDonnel Road to Channing Way. I opened the bedroom drapes to let in the morning light and saw her in the pine tree—black cap, white belly, yellow legs, long white head plumes. She typically visited in late fall and winter, but she arrived early last year when she knew we needed her, standing vigil in her tree, keeping me company while Steve was hospitalized for his final surgery. She came the morning I brought him home too. I settled Steve in our bed—he was so thin, his eyes sunk in black pits, his breathing a trial—and propped him up against the pillows.

"Look," I said, "Big Bird."

He turned to the window. She was perched on a low branch, in the open; no need for binoculars. The smile that spread across Steve's face was so full and light, as if he was momentarily buoyed above his pain by nature's beauty.

He died that night at five forty-six in the evening. Napoleon stood with his front paws on the bed and licked his face, as if knowing that I had neglected to wash Steve's face when I'd bathed him earlier.

The next morning Big Bird was gone.

I didn't see her again until the forty-ninth day after Steve's passing. According to Buddhism, it takes forty-nine days for the Bodhisattva to ready the deceased for rebirth. So Big Bird returned to her pine tree to let me know that Steve's spirit had peacefully settled in his next life. I haven't seen her since, her job done, but I thank her for being here when I needed her in those lonely, frightening, sorrowful days, and for gifting Steve a last smile.

She may have been a different bird each time, but who cares? She is Big Bird, a messenger and carrier of spirits. I know she will be here for me again one day.

A local pro-Communist organization was sponsoring a carnival— mostly propaganda exhibits and plays, folk dances, regional foods. Just about everyone I knew was going.

"My school's participating," I lied to my mother. "Students are required to attend."

I promised to be home by ten o'clock. She said she would send Ah Ying to pick me up at nine-thirty, since the carnival was on the other side of town.

Ah Ying was prompt, but a little stage production I wanted to see, mostly because Chan Pei and Shuet King and the girls they walked home with wanted to see it, hadn't even started yet. Ah Ying was intrigued by the festivities, so it was easy to convince her to stay and watch the play. It was about the life of a farmer on the banks of the Yangtze River. We didn't get back to the cottage until after midnight. My mother was up waiting for me, duster in hand.

"You lied to me," she said.

She knew from #23 Aunt that my school had nothing to do with the carnival. She accused me of wanting to participate in Communist activities.

"You're grounded, except for going to and from school!"

"For how long?"

"Until I say otherwise!"

Ah Ying, failing to smooth things over, gestured for me to kneel down in front of my mother, to admit guilt and apologize. Less concerned about the duster than of being stuck at home until who knew when, I did it—lowered to my knees and asked forgiveness.

"Forgive you?" my mother huffed.

She launched into a lecture. I don't remember her words, only the sense of a long-suffering woman put out by her foolish and intractable daughter. And maybe not only that. My godfather Luther still hadn't come to live with us, remaining in Hong Kong, and my father was hardly ever home. The sole man in my mother's life was a blind octogenarian who thought she could do no right. She went on and on, lecturing me into bed, sitting on the mattress next to me, the unused duster in her hand. One a.m. came and went.

"I'm sorry," I said again, mentally and physically exhausted. "I was wrong. We can talk more about it tomorrow, okay?"

I'm not sure what came over me then, but as my mother sat there, chiding me, so close and yet...

I sat up and tried to hug her.

I suppose I was desperate for a sign that she loved me, a gesture that would keep me from hating myself for causing so much pain and anger, but I should have known better. My mother had never shown me physical affection, not so much as a kiss goodnight.

She pushed me away and stood. I burst out crying.

"Stop that. You'll wake your grandparents."

As if her lecturing hadn't already woken them! I could not stop sobbing.

"Get up," she said. "Go. Now. Leave this house."

I was too beaten down to argue. I crawled from bed and got dressed under her stern eye. She followed to the back door and locked it behind me. *Click*!

I had been "adopted" by a group of older girls by then, its leaders two seventeen-year-olds we called Big Sis and Big Brother. Both of them were already in high school—the same high school I would soon be attending, in the former mansion of some rich Portuguese on the crest of Pine Hill, with a panoramic view of the delta.

Thrown out into the early morning dark, dazed by rejection, I decided to go to Big Sis's house. I was afraid that, even at such a late hour, I might run into Mechanical Man or a pack of Macanese boys or drunk soldiers, and Chan Pei's and Shuet King's houses were too far away.

Big Sis lived alone with her mother. She answered the door herself, surprised to see me—I don't think just because of the hour; I'd never visited her on my own. I explained what had happened and she invited me to stay the night.

I got into Big Sis's bed like so many times before, Chan Pei and Big Brother and I having spent many happy hours there, just lying about and talking.

"No. Under the covers," she said.

She scooted to my side and told me in a tender voice not to worry about the drama with my mother. She brushed my hair with her fingers, wiped away my tears. Her hand ran down my thigh and up across my belly, traced figure eights. I didn't dare say anything, tried not to stiffen or let my breath catch. Big Sis held me as she fell asleep and the hug did feel kind of nice—it was the gesture I hadn't gotten from my mother—but I was also nervous and uncertain and for the longest time I couldn't close my eyes.

"Sis!" Chan Pei called from the street in the morning. She often passed by the house on her way to school, and the two of them would walk partway together. "Sis!"

When Chan Pei heard my news, she said I could stay with her if my mother really was disowning me, and for most of the day I thought I *would*, but by the time classes let out, I'd decided I had to go home for a change of clothes, at the very least.

Big Sis offered to let me spend the night again. "Get some clothes and come over," she said.

No. What had happened in her bed made me too uncomfortable. It might not have been a sexual experience, exactly, but it was still the most physically intimate I'd been with anyone.

At home, while Ah Ying silently poured tea, I knelt down in front of my mother for the second time in as many days. I apologized for lying about the carnival and staying out past my curfew, although I modestly insisted that my misbehavior had nothing to do with an interest in communism and I had only wanted to be with friends.

She coolly lifted a steaming cup to her lips, fluttered a dismissive hand. "I've forgotten all about it," she said.

It pains me to know that I've acted like my mother at her worst. When my elder daughter was two-and-a-half years old, I tried teaching her how to write simple numbers—one, two, three, four, five. She wasn't physically able to do it, and in frustration I took out my rattan duster and beat her twice on the back of the legs. The next day, I saw the red stripes on her toddler legs and felt horrible, vowing not to do anything like that again. And I haven't. She herself doesn't seem to remember the incident; I once heard her tell a friend that I've never hit her.

Another afternoon, I was so fed up with my younger daughter's mess—clothes, dirty and clean, covering the floor of her room so that I couldn't even see the carpet—that I tossed all of it out a window.

"I don't want you living here anymore!" I yelled.

She was five years old. She didn't argue or break out in tears. She simply left and went to her piano teacher's house a few doors down. The teacher, Mrs. Skinner, wasn't home, so she went to a neighbor's across the street.

"I have a little girl here who I think belongs to you," the neighbor Betty phoned to say, at which point the awful recognition came—I had become the last woman I'd ever wanted to be.

I walked over to Betty's house and brought my daughter home, and together we picked up her clothes that were scattered about the driveway.

During an eighth-grade school trip to Hong Kong, a strange noise woke me in the middle of the night—Shuet King, in bed next to me, crying.

"What's wrong? What happened?"

She shook her head.

"Tell me."

"Promise we'll still be friends," she said.

After I did, she confessed that she was in love with me and always wanted to be physically close. Since we were deskmates in class, we often leaned against each other to read a book or complete an assignment. To me, this was a natural expression of two friends, but Shuet King said her heart beat violently every time I touched her, even accidentally. She said she was jealous of Chan Pei. She continued to cry, and I lay there, not sure what to say, mistakenly believing that our friendship wouldn't change, that it hadn't already.

My grandmother would sit meekly by while Ngoi-Gung berated and complained, I said earlier. What I didn't say was that she would afterward go around doing damage-control, mending fences with my mother or Ah Ying or a neighbor, whoever had borne the brunt of my grandfather's wrath; then, weary with effort, she would lie in bed for hours.

But something broke inside her, gave way.

Now whenever my grandfather roused into loudmouthed chagrin, she matched him in volume and said that if he didn't change his attitude, she would indeed divorce him. I doubt she meant it literally; she was seventy-eight years old and had stayed with him despite decades of a hemmed-in life. But for the rest of the time I lived with them, until 1959, the daily scenes were the same—Ngoi-Gung scolding someone, Ngoi-Po threatening divorce if he didn't stop, then mending fences, and afterward lying in bed exhausted.

My daughters, I suspect, feel I didn't nurture them, which is probably true. Oh, I enrolled them in the Girl Scouts and supported their outdoorsy activities. I took them to San Francisco's Chinatown to see how fortune cookies were made, and threw birthday parties for them and bought them their beloved Snoopy dolls. My daughters weren't lacking in *those* kinds of things. But I could have cuddled and cooed over them more, regularly expressed my love for them. I could have provided them with a healthy portion of what I call "emotional nutrition." Steve was better at this, more outwardly affectionate, but he never made a meal for them, bathed them, or changed their diapers.

Had I wanted children? Yes, but mostly because it was what one did—got married and had kids. I had no idea what mother-hood required, what I was *lacking*. I have a lot of capacity to love, I just don't know how to show it. I've done the best I could, given my upbringing and cultural conditioning, so I don't feel a need to apologize, but I regret that I haven't been able to convey the depth of my love for my daughters. The efforts I made before Steve got sick seemed to come too late. I would suggest shopping excursions, meals together, but they didn't happen, my daughters busy with their own lives. My older daughter would check in with me more out of obligation than because she wanted to—that was the sense I had, anyway. And my younger daughter? There was no real intimacy in her visits. She would talk to me as if in perpetual argument, her manner mechanical; she was going through the motions expected of her, in much the same way I once wiped her bottom and gave her a bath.

I wish my relationship with my daughters was like that of a good friend. That it isn't—yes, it's a huge regret, the biggest of my life, and I wonder...

Might our shared grief lead us to a better understanding of one another? Help us form a closer bond? It would be a final, bittersweet gift from Steve.

Dear daughters…

I often think of writing a letter to explain what I find it impossible to say. But am I already writing it? Is *this* it?

Mrs. Tang, my ninth-grade writing teacher, was a widow in her thirties, a favorite of mine and Chan Pei's, and on every assignment we competed for the top grade in her class. She began to give me books and pamphlets to read—*The Communist Manifesto*, Mao's *On New Democracy*, writings on "criticism and self-criticism" and materialism. I was used to fables and fantastical stories, so this wasn't the easiest subject matter for me to absorb as a thirteen-year-old. But I came to understand some of it, to enjoy the challenge of trying to understand it, especially since Mrs. Tang met with me once a week after school to ask if I had any questions about what I read. It was from her that I learned of a people's responsibility to their country and vice versa, as well as of people's responsibility to one another.

"The class system and materialism are evils," she said, and talked of the ongoing struggle to free China from feudal, colonial structures and corruption. "Do you know what communism is?" She herself answered before I could. "An antidote to the social and economic and political problems of the country, if not the world."

I was receptive, willing to entertain anything if it meant Mrs. Tang would keep being nice to me. Her patience, the modest and reasonable way she talked with me—they reminded me of Auntie Amy. But also, the idea of a just society, a society in which people were less selfish and always awake to the common good, naturally appealed to me. I didn't ask Mrs. Tang who determined the common good. By what authority? And I didn't admit that I balked at communism's rejection of an individual's feelings, at how none of us was supposed to be attached to friends and family, only to the global ideal of a world without suffering and inequity. Emotional attachments to others was a weakness, Mrs. Tang said, hindering one's effectiveness as a fighter in the people's liberation because it rendered one less than utterly committed to the cause. Which made communism not very different from a cult.

Mrs. Tang invited me to her house for dinner. She lived the life of a proletariat; the food was simple, not plentiful. She had a six-year-old daughter prone to illness, and if anyone had asked me what I thought after seeing the two of them together—their rapport, their laughter—I would have said that Mrs. Tang seemed extremely attached to her daughter and I wished I had a mother like her.

"What I've observed of you this year has been quite impressive," she said to me once we were alone after dinner. "Have you ever considered joining the Komsomol?"

She assumed that I knew about the underground Communist youth organization. I had heard about it from Chan Pei, who became dramatically whispery whenever, with equal parts awe and longing, she mentioned it. But no, I had never considered trying to join.

"Technically, you're too young," Mrs. Tang said. "You're supposed to be fourteen, but since you've proven what you can do intellectually and shown leadership in class...if you *are* interested, I could be your sponsor. In fact, I've already recommended you. It's strictly voluntary, and if you don't like it, you can leave at any time."

Had she recommended Chan Pei? Had she been giving books to

Chan Pei too, discussing them with her after school? I hadn't told my friend about the extra attention I was getting, protective of it.

"I'm not from the working class or a peasant family," I reminded Mrs. Tang, and not just because of my parents' education and our maids. My father had a new business growing Hawaiian papaya on a farm outside Kowloon, selling the crop in an increasing number of major fruit markets in and around Hong Kong.

"The bourgeois are represented in the stars of the Chinese flag," she said.

There I was, having never felt connected to anything, having never considered myself worthy of importance, and I had a chance to join a pioneering movement sweeping through China and possibly the world.

"You don't need to decide now. Think it over," Mrs. Tang advised. "I'm confident that what we've talked about today will remain between us."

"Yes," I said in understanding: despite blatant Communist propaganda, Macau was a Portuguese colony after all, the Komsomol underground.

I considered the offer for two weeks while reading a book Mrs. Tang gave me, a novel called *How the Steel Was Tempered* about a handicapped Russian worker who struggled against great odds to lead a revolution and sacrifice his life for the Party and his country. My years of sickness, my unhappy relationship with my mother, my father's lengthy absences—none of it compared with what Paul, the book's main character, experienced. I reproached myself for my self-pity. I decided that I needed to be attached to something worthwhile, to have a purpose larger than myself—like working to raise the social conscience of other young people, to impart to them the importance of worldwide liberation from materialism, fortifying our generation's commitment to forming a classless society. I applied to the Komsomol under the name Perseverance, claiming that I would persevere in the struggle and ultimate victory of the people. In the late spring of 1952, I was admitted as one of its youngest members.

I met with Mrs. Tang every week, usually at her house, and we talked a lot about the Korean War, what the Korean soldiers and People's Army were risking to defend against the US invasion.

"More American lives have been lost than the press is reporting," she said. "The people of Korea will ultimately win since it's their country and their heritage they're fighting for."

I thought Korea should have been left alone to settle their own internal differences. Greed has no mercy, the Komsomol taught me, and in coming years I would despise the Portuguese and British—colonizers who had no right to be in China, thousands of miles from their own countries, at best treating indigenous populations like third-class citizens. But curiously, I never entertained the same antipathy toward America or lost my desire to come here.

The summer before high school, Chan Pei was more explicitly pro-Communist than ever. She wanted to follow my brother Bentham's example—leave Westernized Macau and return to China proper to study.

"They won't let me," she said of her parents. "They'll disown me if I go."

I didn't tell her that I was glad, that I didn't want to lose her again. But then I remembered: as a Komsomol member, I had responsibilities. In the army for liberation, I was expected to encourage and recruit others to join the cause. I came up with a plan. If Chan Pei was serious about escaping her home and family, I knew how she could get the money to do it.

"How?" she asked.

"We pretend to see movies a few times a week and you keep the money your mother gives you until you have enough for a train ticket and expenses."

"You'll help me do that?"

"It's what you want, isn't it—to go?"

This was as explicit as I ever got about being in the Komsomol, and Chan Pei didn't push for more. Her parents never suspected our deceit. At the end of the summer she bought a train ticket to Canton, where, through Mrs. Tang, arrangements had been made for her to rendezvous with a comrade. I went to her house the night before she left and smuggled out clothes and a few belongings that she'd be taking with her, which I carried home, on the watch for #23 Aunt. Since Ah Ying was proletariat, I'd told her I was Komsomol, and she helped me pack Chan Pei's things for the next morning, when, again on the lookout for #23 Aunt, I met my friend at the train station.

It was like our first parting in Canton years earlier. I was unable to look at her, panicked and nauseated. *Never give yourself away under duress*, the Komsomol taught. In difficult situations, I was to think about all those who had lost their lives for the revolution, how each time I helped someone join the cause, I was getting closer to the goal of liberating the people. So I tried to focus on those things as I watched Chan Pei board the train, but I couldn't help feeling guilt mixed in with my sadness. Had helping my friend been the right course of action? I later heard that she was sent to a remote province of Gansu, in north central China, where she became a doctor's assistant, then married the doctor and had two children. But this doesn't tell me if the life Chan Pei chose proved satisfactory to her, or if she ever talked to her parents once she had left Macau.

After watching her board the train that long-ago morning, I immediately left to attend my first day of high school, and was never in touch with her again.

5

WE DIDN'T HAVE A REFRIGERATOR, and two or three times a day Ah Ying had to go food shopping. The market was ten minutes from the cottage, but being social, she was often gone for more than an hour, and my mother became distrustful.

"From now on, you're to write down everything you buy and how much it cost," she said.

It *was* common for cooks or maids to take advantage of the haggling at the market—paying, for example, $3.50 for a pound of pork, but claiming that the best bargain to be had was $5.00 and pocketing the difference.

"Everything you buy, and for what price," my mother insisted. "In writing."

But Ah Ying, it turned out, was illiterate. So every night at the tiny desk I'd rigged up in the storage space where I slept, my mother listened to her oral reports on what groceries she had bought that day, from whom, and for how much. My mother wrote everything down, asking questions to be sure of Ah Ying's absolute honesty, and frequently going to the market the following day to confirm what she'd been told.

My desk. I was spending countless hours there, writing papers on political pamphlets as part of my training in the Komsomol. Because my mother never asked what I was working on, it had been easy to keep her in ignorance of my Communist associations. Had she even noticed I'd become more studious? Who knows? But I tend to think *not*, otherwise why did she commandeer my desk when she could have used the dining table?

"You can learn to read and write," I said to Ah Ying.

"No, I'm too old."

"I'll teach you. Do you *like* being interrogated every night?"

She could soon write down what groceries she bought, for how much, and from whom. But what she really wanted, she confessed, was to be able to write a letter home.

Ah Ying had been twenty-nine when she started working for my family. She came from a region south of Canton, she explained, where they raised silkworms. She said that only young women worked in the silkworm farms and factories, but if one didn't want to work in those environments, if one was sick of silkworms and wished to leave for the city, then first she had to get married so that the elders would consider her safe from corruption and agree to let her go. Evidently, many women never returned or remarried, although they continued to send money home. Staying married like that made no sense to me, but Ah Ying was one of these women. When she confessed that she would like to write a letter to her parents and husband, I finally understood why this attractive young woman in good health always shook her head *no, no* every time my mother talked to her about marrying. I agreed to continue tutoring her.

The Komsomol recognized my work with Ah Ying as a model for how the bourgeois class could help the proletariat. Mrs. Tang repeatedly praised my dedication to the people's liberation. But my motivation had been selfish. Tired of my mother quizzing a maid in my sleeping area night after night, I had figured if Ah Ying could write her own shopping reports, then it would stop and I'd get my desk back.

Dear daughters,

It has been more than a year since your dad died and you know that I have gone from crying uncontrollably to freaking out at trivialities. Never have I felt so helpless and needy, which I don't like to acknowledge even though I know I shouldn't care and it is considered unsurprising for someone who has lost her husband of thirty-five years. Some of my shame comes from wishing I could have spared you my behavior, since you have your own grieving to do. Daughters whose father recently died of cancer don't need to hear their mother wish for the courage to commit suicide.

One of my favorite movies, you may not know, stars William Holden and Jennifer Jones. It's called *Love Is a Many-Splendored Thing*. As the plot of the movie suggests, however, even Hollywood knows that love is more of a many-*splintered* thing—part joy, pain, happiness, frustration, and anger. These emotions rarely surface at the same time or in equal proportion, and the love we three share has maybe been more pain and frustration than joy. But I remember when you each took your first steps, uttered your first words, attended your first day of kindergarten. Your father and I were so happy, we cried.

Please know my love for you is abundant. I have always been proud of your achievements, big and small, even though I have not communicated this sufficiently to you.

Sometimes we unwittingly resist what we most desire. I have done so—I can admit that. One day, I hope you will find it easier to accept me, faults and all. One day, I hope you will come to look at me differently, although I may be largely the same person I am now—a loving mother who even in grief doesn't feel quite free with you, but then I don't feel free with anybody and so you shouldn't take it personally. I have done what I could with what I had. I am trying to be a better person for you, and I hope I have not caused more misunderstanding by writing this.

XOXO

The Komsomol—yes, I felt connected to something larger than myself and experienced a sense of belonging to a degree I had never known. And I like to think that all those papers I wrote for my training or indoctrination or whatever people might call it improved my critical thinking and helped me excel in school. Also, my work in the organization gave me a good grounding in psychology, which is ironic since Communists claim not to believe in it. By "psychology" I mean that I learned how to influence people, how to spot and exploit weakness in others, just as it had been spotted in me—a somewhat alienated girl who needed to feel a deeper connection to the world. Did the Komsomol teach me to be good at keeping secrets? No, I was already good at that.

The problem was, I lost my teens to the serious business of revolution. While other girls my age enjoyed bike rides along the banks of the delta, reading comics, spending entire afternoons being silly or mischievous, I was hunched at my desk writing papers that improved my critical thinking, turning myself into a role model in order to gain the trust of the people.

"I'm sorry," Mrs. Tang said, because the Komsomol was assigning me a new supervisor. "It would be suspicious for us to continue. Now that you're in high school and we don't see each other in class every day, there's no apparent reason for us to be friends."

And I had joined partly so that she would keep caring for me!

We met in the Catholic cemetery, my new supervisor and I, by the gravestone of a Portuguese general whose name I don't remember. The place was a tourist attraction and it wasn't unusual for people to visit in the afternoon and walk around looking at headstones.

"We want you to get elected to student government," she said.

She was a woman in her late twenties, rather plain-looking, clipped and efficient in her manner.

"It's a way for you to wield more influence with your schoolmates."

I thought I was best suited for Student Editorial Chief, who was responsible for putting out a weekly bulletin.

"Ah, that's good," she said.

A comrade was being assigned to me for supervision, I learned.

I would meet her in the cemetery in a few days. How specifically I was to instruct this person, I wasn't told. I would find out if she had read all the materials I'd been given and start there, I decided.

In the twenty-odd times I met with my new superior, she never confided her name or anything else about herself, but from the ugly, thick-soled shoes she wore, I assumed she was a nurse at the hospital. According to Mrs. Tang, several members of the Komsomol worked there, and I eventually came to suspect it was the organization's HQ; when I had my appendix removed, I was tested under anesthetic, blurry people around my bed asking whether I knew anything about the Komsomol and if I was a member.

After six months, with no warning, I was assigned a new supervisor—again, a woman in her late twenties who never confided her name but who didn't wear thick, ugly shoes. She simply showed up at the Portuguese general's grave when I was expecting her predecessor.

Occasionally, I passed Mrs. Tang on the street and she greeted me as if I were merely a former student of hers, nothing more.

Kids at my school who supported the Nationalist government in Taiwan were generally from the bourgeoisie and those in favor of the Communists tended to be working class. When I started my campaign to become Student Editorial Chief, I was surprised to find that the progressive students were all for me while the pro-Nationalists were split. But because the Editor was required to sit in on different classes in order to write about them, and a number of boys wanted more opportunities to talk to me, they gave me their votes and I was elected. Under my leadership, the slant of the weekly bulletin became moderately progressive, in accord with the atmosphere at the time, but never anti-Nationalist.

"Make it more progressive," my supervisor instructed at the cemetery.

But hadn't I been chosen by the Komsomol because, as a member of the bourgeoisie, no one would publicly suspect me of being in it? Which meant I could exert influence subtly rather than too openly and dogmatically to change anyone's mind.

My supervisor took that back to her colleagues. They agreed with me and the slant of the bulletin remained moderate. It was my first taste of politics outside my own family and further taught me the importance of compromise and diplomacy.

There had to be others but I never met them and they remained figments—I mean other Komsomol members besides Chui, the girl I supervised and rendezvoused with once a week among the gravestones.

"American casualties aren't as high as the press is reporting," I said, echoing what Mrs. Tang had told me about the Korean War.

We discussed the heroism of Communist forces during the Long March of the 1930s, when they had trekked thousands of kilometers from the southeast, over mountains and across rivers, fighting Chiang Kai-shek's army the entire way to Shaanxi, where Mao firmly established his position as Party leader.

"I'm thinking of going to the USSR to learn Russian," she said.

I encouraged her. I had been given a lot of literature that glorified the USSR's partnership with China in communism, and I passed along what I had to her. Chui was a few years older than me and out of high school. No one had instructed me to give her an assignment—whatever might have been the equivalent, for her, of getting elected to student government. I didn't tell her anything about myself. I had the feeling she'd been sent to watch me. Paranoia was cultivated by the Communists so that we wouldn't trust one another, only the Party.

"No man will be interested in you," my mother used to say, unaware of the soldiers in movie theatres who didn't share her opinion. "You're not feminine enough."

But by the age of fourteen, I was routinely finding notes from secret admirers in my desk drawer at school. And less shy boys started visiting me at home—some pro-Nationalist government, others Communists. My mother gave the Communists a pass, thankful for their interest in her only daughter.

"So you might not wind up an old maid, after all," she said, "but the next time Deming comes over, it wouldn't hurt you to be a little more quiet and reserved."

Deming played the trumpet. He was a Nationalist. He came to the cottage one morning, more neatly dressed than usual and without his trumpet case.

Would I be his date to an upcoming school dance? he asked.

I was elated. I very much wanted to accept, to say *yes, yes* to my first date with a boy I had a crush on, but the image of Mrs. Tang swam up before me. Komsomol members weren't supposed to have boyfriends or girlfriends, and they certainly weren't allowed to be close to anyone outside the organization, let alone a Nationalist. As overly dramatic as it might sound, I felt that I had no freedom to explore my affections, to love.

"I'm sorry, no," I told Deming.

"What?" my mother said in appalled disbelief when she heard. "Why didn't you accept?"

Because I couldn't tell her the real reason, I was never able to satisfactorily explain myself

Steve, I never regretted my choice.

A wealthy man would not have suited me, would have allowed me to be dependent, pampered, useless. Yes, I had my opportunities, as he knew, which was why he said he worked hard to give me what I might have had. But what might I have had? Despite the frustrations and compromises inevitable in a long marriage, I got much more with him.

I do wish he hadn't been ashamed of his humble background, though. It was as if he feared that to be otherwise might have allowed poverty to sneak up and overtake him again. Tirelessly, relentlessly he worked to distance himself from the first seven years of his life—six in the village, one in Canton after the war—when he and his mother were alone, waiting until his father, a soldier under Patton, could arrange for them to join him in Los Angeles; distance himself too from those years after his arrival in the US, when he gradually picked up bits and pieces of the foreign tongue that surrounded him; when he slept among fruit crates in South Central and helped in his father's store, first by organizing Coke bottles for recycling and stacking groceries, then after his English was good enough, by taking over the ordering of groceries and helping with the customers and suppliers. And all the while, his father blamed him whenever anything went wrong, from a radio not working to a shipment of canned goods being delayed, and reserved his kindness for the children who came in for free candy. Tirelessly, relentlessly, Steve strove. He was the first in his family to go to college.

I knew, when we first met, that he was one of those immigrants looking to marry someone fluent in Cantonese, wanting a wife capable of talking with his parents, neither of whom had grown comfortable using English.

"I'm a Communist," he joked after introducing himself at the USC library.

He drew a picture—of me. We were the same age, but he was an undergraduate, studying architecture after having transferred from UCLA, where he had been pre-med to please his parents. He was good at drawing. I kept the picture he did of me.

Our courtship lasted two-and-a-half years, during which Steve perfected his skills in the art and science of architecture and continued to help at the family store. Encouraged by a close friend from the same village, Steve's father Harold had expanded the store, he and his wife Mary overseeing the produce and dry goods sections while renting out the meat and seafood counters to others.

"Yes, but only after I graduate," I said when I agreed to marry Steve.

Six months later, on a Thursday, I received my diploma. We exchanged our vows the following Sunday—on January 28th, 1962—at two-thirty, because Auntie Lily wanted the hour hand of the clock going up, not down. Steve's parents worked at their store until two, then drove to the Presbyterian church in West Hollywood, where the ceremony was being held. Auntie Lily regularly worshipped there, and she'd had the chapel decorated with white flowers and ribbons. I wore a dress I'd bought at I.Magnin, the least expensive I could find, onto which I'd sewn fake pearls from J.C. Penny.

My parents couldn't afford to attend, but they celebrated in Hong Kong at a restaurant—six tables full of friends and relatives, including Ngoi-Gung and Ngoi-Po, Auntie Fong, Auntie Doris, and Uncle Ernest.

In Los Angeles, there were two receptions: one at the church in the afternoon and another that night, in Chinatown—a traditional Chinese banquet hosted by Steve's parents. They finally had the opportunity to repay the social debts they felt they owed to friends and relatives who had hosted such celebrations for their own children and nieces and nephews over the years. We took up two restaurants because no single restaurant was large enough to accommodate the entire party—forty-four tables' worth of guests. Thirty-five tables were filled by people invited by Steve's parents. The other nine were for my and Steve's friends—professors and fellow students from USC. I wore a new outfit—a black-and-red *cheongsam* with seven-inch slits at the sides and a matching jacket with three-quarter-length sleeves, which my mother had commissioned from a Shanghainese tailor in Hong Kong and mailed to me. Steve and I didn't even have time to eat dinner; we were too busy running between the restaurants all night, mingling with our guests, and then I had to perform the evening's tea ceremony in honor of my new mother-in-law.

A new bride, I had $400 to my name.

Never in all the months leading to my wedding, never in all the years afterward, did I tell Steve: his scrappy background was attractive to me. We had both traveled far from the country of our birth— we would, as equals, make our own way together.

I mostly kept my feelings to myself as a teenager, a reticence that I believe stemmed from the lack of nurturing I received when younger. I had grown up like a famished child who got her nutrition sporadically—just enough to keep her alive and hungry. Also, people had been coming and going from my life for as long as I could remember. Chan Pei had flitted through twice. Big Sister and Big Brother were busy with their nurses' training. Tsang Shuet King, who wasn't in my high school class and whom I rarely saw, belonged mostly to the past, as did Mrs. Tang. The result? Whenever I met someone new, I anticipated our future separation and, in order to lessen any pain when parting, held myself emotionally aloof. But not with Chi Chiang...

He was slender, with thick eyebrows and hair parted to the side. The mysteriously quiet type, he reminded me of Montgomery Clift. In biology class, we were assigned as partners to catch specific varieties of butterflies for a project. I don't exactly remember what we talked about on our excursions, only that when I was with him I felt easy and relaxed and my reticence fell away. Not completely, but more than it ever had with a boy. He told me I was smart and pretty. I didn't dare mention him to my Komsomol supervisor, although she probably knew about our relationship. In any case, she didn't ask about him and we let my biology project be my excuse for spending time with him.

Chi Chiang and I started going to the Cape of the Wandering Soul on our butterfly hunts, a sort of lover's lane. It was near the end of a narrow serpentine road, just past a sharp turn where many inattentive drivers had had head-on collisions or driven off the cliff, their deaths giving the spot its name. Still, it was a beautiful place, with something of the eternal in its ever-shifting landscape, and before long Chi Chiang and I weren't doing much in the way of catching butterflies. We would sit in some discreet spot, other couples tucked from sight nearby, and gaze out over the delta with its sparkling water and small nearby islands.

"Do you know why boys like to visit you?" he teasingly asked.

"Because I'm smart and pretty?"

"You don't wear a bra."

I told him about my experiment with Auntie Amy's chest binders and how I hadn't liked wearing bras after that.

Another time, butterfly nets over our shoulders, we were walking to the cape to enjoy the sunset when we were swiped by a speeding car. I woke up in the hospital with a broken leg. My mother was there.

"Chi Chiang?" I asked.

She shook her head.

He'd been walking nearest the road and had died at the scene. My father briefly returned from Hong Kong, but what could he do? I remained in a daze. I felt as if I were looking out at the world from a small window in a detached room, forced to watch people and doings that were alien to me. Never physically robust, I was more self-conscious than usual, hobbling around with a broken leg. My school work flagged. My periods, which had been getting worse every year, were lasting for ten days or more, and I was sick of spending two afternoons a week in a cemetery. I couldn't sleep and started to suffer from migraines.

"STOP THAT! STOP! What are you doing?"

My mother had walked in on me banging my head against the wall—the only way I could get relief from my migraines.

She took me to a series of doctors, one of whom discovered that

I had a leaky heart valve and said I should be excused from all P.E. activities, which was funny, given what my mother had studied. The leaky valve had nothing to do with my migraines, of course, and I don't know whether it was psychosomatic or not, but after my diagnosis, the slightest physical exertion gave me chest pains and left me short of breath. So did thinking about how I no longer wanted to be political but was afraid to quit the Komsomol, believing harm would come to me or my family, and how I wanted to go somewhere far away on my magic carpet, to enjoy my youth, my life—as I had with Chi Chiang.

I had an appointment with my gynecologist today.

"You lost weight!" she said.

The last time I saw her I weighed 114 pounds. This visit, with similar clothing, only ninety-six. Am I trying to put Jenny Craig out of business? I wouldn't recommend my diet to anyone.

Dr. O'Reilly always takes time to ask after me, aware of my hardships both in having cared for Steve and in mourning him. She suggested I get my primary care doctor to scan my abdomen. Sometimes a tumor in the pancreas causes weight loss like mine. Thank you, Doctor, that's all I need: a cancerous tumor. But if I have pancreatic cancer—forgive me, my daughters—I will let it be.

Steve once said that he didn't have to live a long life, that if he could walk his two daughters down the aisle and make it to, say, the age of seventy, he would be satisfied. He did neither.

I feel like I am too old to start anything new, too young to die.

My in-laws wanted us to live with them after we married.

"I'd rather not," I said. "I don't want them to pay for your education anymore either."

Steve's face wrinkled in confusion.

"I'll pay for it," I said.

With my MSW newly in hand, I had been hired by the International Institute of Los Angeles as a liaison for Chinese families. I was the Institute's first Chinese employee. My salary was $300 a month—not a lot in 1962.

How did Steve's parents react, hearing that we wouldn't be moving in with them? He never said, but I read their resentment in the way they wouldn't quite look at me when we were together, addressing me with as few words as possible. No doubt this resentment was also the result of another refusal: I hadn't wanted to take my husband's surname—a practice I considered sexist, demeaning. But the decision to invent a new surname was both mine and Steve's, a compromise. Many people working in Los Angeles architecture were named Wong and he wasn't excited to add to their number. Wong: a name called near the end of an alphabetical sequence, a caboose.

"Why do you want to change it?" Steve's parents kept asking, not understanding.

They knew there was no point in vehemently objecting; our minds were made up. But we invented a new name that doesn't exist in Cantonese. In China, my daughters and I are still Wongs.

As to the hurt my in-laws felt over Steve and I not moving in with them...

"We wanted to help our only son," Harold eventually admitted. I was alone with him in the Palos Verdes house that he and Mary had bought upon retirement. "But we both understand your decision now, and we respect you for it."

It was one of the strongest bonds we had, Steve and I—our drive to be economically independent and secure.

Although I was almost fifteen years old, my mother still beat me whenever she thought I was out of line.

"Why are you late?" she asked.

She had met me at the door, the rattan duster in her fist. Ngoi-Gung had been particularly quarrelsome and nitpicky with her all day, I figured.

"I come home around this time at least twice a week," I said, in a mood myself because, again, I was tired of Macau and the Komsomol.

She didn't like my tone and raised her arm to hit me. I snatched the duster out of her hand and broke it in half and threw it on the floor.

"Never again," I said, pointing at it. "The next time you try, I'll beat *you*."

Open-mouthed, she said nothing, and for the first time I understood that I had control over what happened to me.

I am tempted to qualify what I relate of my mother, not wanting her to appear wholly cruel and hateful. But qualify how? My memories are, to my mind, true. I recollect them honestly, it's just that they somehow leave out important factors. Also, I don't feel as harshly toward her as I once did. Why am I afraid to plainly acknowledge our lifelong tussle? The answer, I think, is a daughter's love, my instinct as a daughter to love my mother as much as I can. And as I continue to try and rise above my own failings, I would rather not resent her just because she never seemed to make a similar effort. Which I guess is another way of saying that I would like to be as generous toward her as I hope my daughters will be to me.

And yet...and yet...

In public my mother remained a Mrs. Good—hospitable and generous with friends and neighbors, willing to do anything for them, always making sure there was tea in their cups and that they had enough to eat when she entertained them at the cottage. I came to view her as a non-person, a woman concerned only with the frilly things of life, with no opinions of her own about serious issues.

"I don't understand why all my friends like me and you're the only one who doesn't," she commented to me.

"Well, I don't understand why my friends like *me* but you don't," I countered, although who my friends were just then, it would have been hard for me to say.

That was as deep as we ever got about our relationship.

Not brave enough to try the duster on me again, my mother increased her nagging. If I accidentally broke a dish, she harangued me about all the dishes I'd broken since I was two. If I left a shirt on the floor, she went on and on about how she could have twenty maids and it wouldn't be enough to clean up after me. Constant nagging was a doubtful improvement over periodic beatings, so I kept away from the cottage as much as I could. And when I was home, I acted out more. Returning for lunch one day, the maid didn't answer the door fast enough and I put my fist through the glass. My mother froze, frightened by the blood. Ah Ying hurried to get wet cloths and bandages. I stood heaving, short of breath, the injured hand belonging to someone else.

In the summer of 1953, shortly after the armistice was signed and hostilities in Korea ceased (the war goes on, but not the mortal combat), my mother and I took a steamship to Hong Kong to visit my father, where, since 1949, he'd been spending most of every year. During our stay, we met up with Luther, who was living in the city with his older brother's family. We learned that he was in the process of moving to Pakistan.

"Karachi?" my mother said, her porcelain brow cracking.

My father puffed at his cigarette. It was evidently old news to him.

Luther and his elder brother were opening a match factory in Karachi and had been preparing to relocate, but the brother had suddenly died. The sister-in-law and four nephews had therefore become Luther's responsibility. In order to handle things legally, my godfather had decided to marry his sister-in-law and adopt her kids.

"This is not uncommon in Jiangxi," he said, referring to his native province.

Luther Chang: always a businessman first, a man who sought expediency in everything. Unlike my father, who was more of an idealist, but one who had known of his best friend's looming marriage and hadn't felt the need to mention it to my mother.

Over the previous four years, she had made only occasional trips to Hong Kong, presumably to see her husband. How much could have been going on between her and Luther? Still, my godfather's impending nuptials must have put an end, in her mind, to any possibility of a different life for herself, no matter how unlikely. I have often tried to imagine how she felt when we left Canton, not for Hong Kong as originally intended but for Macau because it was supposedly better for my grandparents' well-being. That decision separated her from Luther, who had been living with us since before I was born. Yes, it must have been hard, to leave him in order to care for her troubled parents.

"This isn't uncommon in Jiangxi," Luther said of his impending marriage, and I, if not my mother, wondered if he had been having an affair with his sister-in-law while his brother was alive, marrying her as soon as the opportunity presented, as he might have done with *her* if circumstances had allowed.

It was my last year in high school and a number of my classmates intended to go to Hong Kong to further their education—the boys at universities, technical or business schools; the girls, to study nursing or, like Shuet King, become teachers. My parents decided that I would attend university, which was the one thing that, despite being rare for girls, my mother didn't consider tomboyish. Why did I let them decide my immediate future for me? I prefer to think it was less because I was a still-young daughter and that's how things were done culturally than because my goals aligned with theirs. Hong Kong wasn't as far away from Macau as I might have liked, but it was my birthplace and a big city—a more likely launch point, I hoped, for a magic carpet ride than the parochial little Portuguese colony.

"You've been a good model for your peers and invaluable to the Party," my Komsomol supervisor said. "I'm sure you will continue to do well there."

She instructed me to apply to the Chinese University rather than the University of Hong Kong because I could then exert more influence. HKU had been established by the British and many of its students had aristocratic backgrounds or were firmly Nationalist or pro-West, whereas Chung Chi College had a good mixture of students from Southeast Asia who were more likely to have Communist sympathies. Once enrolled, my supervisor said, I would be connected with a new chain of command, and I would become eligible for full membership in the Communist Party even though I was only sixteen. Normally, the minimum age was eighteen.

"You should be honored to become one of our youngest full members, and in a leadership capacity too, helping shepherd China into a classless society at the forefront of worldwide liberation."

But Hong Kong was much more pro-Nationalist than Macau, she warned, and there was a lot of espionage, so I had to be careful. My new contact would find me within a month of my arrival there.

I was torn. I wanted to quit the Komsomol but had made a commitment. *Don't be selfish*, I thought. Could I still serve the people if I wasn't a Communist Party member? Could I have the same determination to help the sick and suffering, the poor and oppressed? Shadowing these questions was the old worrying one: Would the Komsomol even let me quit?

Although I hated Macau—the Macanese boys, the soldiers, the Mechanical Man—now that I was leaving it, I became wistful. As long as I was in the colony, I would see Mrs. Tang at least once in a while, but after I was gone...? My feelings for her were mixed, however: I felt a strong affection for her and considered her a mentor, but I wasn't sure if she liked me for *me*, or only because she'd wanted to recruit me into the Komsomol.

Tolerance. This is a big concept in Chinese culture. Instead of divorce, quitting, severing or otherwise putting an end to a situation, you try to find a solution that renders it tolerable. People in China always say, "Let's see what we can do," instead of crying "forget it!" and giving up.

What did I want to do with my life? When I left for Hong Kong in 1955, I knew only that I wanted the freedom to make friends, to date, to go to whatever movie I chose, to write or talk about anything I wished. I would work as hard as necessary to achieve this freedom, I promised myself. Fear and uncertainty wouldn't cause me to cry "forget it!" and give up, but also—tolerance be damned.

6

A YEAR BEFORE STEVE'S DIAGNOSIS, I had a dream. We were with our younger daughter, driving up a coastal road toward a brown house. Out the driver's side windows, on a beach with dark sand, I saw a black-haired man—shirtless, in shorts, lying face-down in the surf. Somehow, I knew he was Chinese.

"When a wave comes in, he's going to be washed away and die," Steve said. "I have to save him,"

"No, don't," I said.

With that lack of transition common to dreams, my daughter and I were then in the brown house. Not Steve. I assumed he had gone to try and save the man and I went to the window and looked down toward the beach. It was deserted. We waited and waited but Steve never came back, and suddenly the light flashed so bright it hurt my eyes and made them water. I found myself alone, looking at a bunch of fish as if I were standing before a huge tank at an aquarium. A whale swam by with Steve holding on to its tail. He climbed onto the animal's back and rode it away from me, out toward the deep wide ocean, and I woke up with tears on my face.

At a loss how to interpret all of this, I forgot about it until after Steve and I took a trip to China, where he got a bad stomachache, which we thought was caused by food-borne parasites. Herbal medicines didn't help, and by the time we were back in the States, he also had a persistent case of hiccups. He went three weeks without a diagnosis. Finally, a CT scan showed an obstruction in his small intestine and he was scheduled for surgery to find out what it was. In the waiting room during the procedure, scared, hardly able to think, I found myself staring at fish in an aquarium. Just as I was remembering my dream, the surgeon emerged from the operating room and told me that Steve had stage-IV colon cancer.

"Unfortunately," he said, "it's metastasized to the stomach lining."

What? I didn't immediately understand. Couldn't. Refused.

Dr. Irving, the oncologist, gave my husband nine months to live, estimating that he'd had cancer for a year, which meant it had started around the time of my dream.

Steve fought and lasted fifteen months. The girls and I scattered some of his ashes in the lagoon, in the shadow of Big Bird's tree. I've kept another small portion to be scattered in the Yangtze River, at a spot that any local boatman will know—the site of the temple honoring Zhang Fei, a general and warrior in the third century who was said to have been the equal of ten thousand men. As a boy, Steve had marched around his village, flag in hand, pretending to be Zhang Fei. The temple formerly commanded a view from a hillside in Chongqing, but the area encompassing it, which included many cities, towns and villages, was flooded when the Three Gorges Dam reservoir became operational. Meant to showcase China's modernization, this dam was touted as protecting downstream communities from seasonal flooding, which could be quite severe, yet people remained—until the Communists forcibly relocated millions of them.

The rest of Steve's ashes the girls and I offered to the bay. We drove to the Marin Headlands in Sausalito, parked at Fort Cronkhite, and followed a path down past cow lilies and cypress trees to Bonita Cove. To our east: the Golden Gate Bridge. To the south: San Francisco. The Pacific spread out before us to the west. Ice plants bloomed pink and dusty yellow beneath the lighthouse. We walked across the dark sand of a little beach, toward the east end of the cove.

"It looks like a puppy sitting there," my younger daughter said, nodding toward a boulder at the base of Point Bonita.

"Like Napoleon," my elder daughter said.

I took the lid off the urn, and there, within a heron's short glide of the Golden Gate, aware that Steve had been the man lying face-down in the surf I'd dreamed about, I said goodbye to most of his earthly remains.

The initial plan was for me and my mother to move to Hong Kong while my grandparents remained in Macau under the care of Ah Ying and another maid. Flats were expensive and hard to get and my mother doubted we would find a suitable place for everyone. But Ah Ying refused to stay with my grandparents, and not wanting to lose her after six years of service, my mother relented and let her come with us.

We were unable to find a small flat of our own and so rented a room that came with a pair of mattresses on the floor against the wall on either side, with drapes hanging along the front of them for privacy. Ah Ying slept in the hallway, on a foldup canvas cot. I don't know how many people lived in this communal flat in the North Point neighborhood; so many were always coming and going. If Ngoi-Gung and Ngoi-Po had been with us, I've no doubt they would have pined for the relatively spacious cottage in Macau the same way they had for the apartment in Canton, never mind their mansion in Nanjing, but I myself was too excited to care about our reduced circumstances. My first night in Hong Kong, I dressed in a white cotton top, pink shorts, and sneakers—everything American-made—and went out for a walk, to feel the energy of the city.

A note came from my comrade superior, my last supervisor in Macau: in a week, at such and such a time, I was to meet my Komsomol connection in a park located at a busy intersection. I was given only her approximate age and a vague physical description; she would recognize me and make the initial contact. But at the park, no one tapped me on the shoulder or engaged me in conversation and I left after an hour. Almost a month passed before I received another note telling me to be at a ferry landing in Kowloon at a certain time on an upcoming day, with no explanation for why I had been stood up at the park.

If I don't leave the Komsomol now, I thought, *I might never. I'll be inducted into the Communist Party for life.*

Determined to quit, I purposely missed the meet at the ferry. I didn't contact anyone afterward either, and waited with no little trepidation to find out what would be done to me.

One reason I chose to attend Chung Chi College instead of Hong Kong University: my less than astounding language skills. I was under the impression that HKU taught strictly in English, with Chinese offered as an elective, while Chung Chi was the reverse. Although both my parents spoke English, my proficiency had largely come from watching Hollywood movies. I could hold a friendly conversation well enough, but following academic lectures and writing papers? I was insecure and didn't think my English would be up to it. Imagine my surprise then, when many of my classes were taught in English. I suppose I should have expected it, really; Chung Chi was a Christian school, founded by Protestants, and a good number of its professors were missionaries and ministers from the US and Canada.

In the 1960s, my alma mater became part of CUHK, the Chinese University of Hong Kong. It is a half-hour's train ride from downtown Kowloon, on a hill overlooking Tolo Harbor—340 acres of paths meandering among buildings in both Chinese and Western architectural styles. But in the spring of 1955, it was a new campus with a rural village atmosphere. There were a couple of small restaurant huts that catered to students and an old villa where the groundskeeper's family lived. The dorms were under construction, making Chung Chi essentially a commuter school my freshman year, with everyone always hurrying after classes to catch buses that would take them home, because the new train station hadn't opened yet. In what little socializing there was, people grouped together according to personal geography and history—the local high school they had attended, whether they came from Malaysia, Singapore or Indonesia, or were the first in their families to go to college. There was a small contingent from Macau, four boys I knew, but I didn't have any classes with them. Were students from the southeast generally sympathetic to communism, as my Komsomol supervisor had claimed? I have no idea. I found it hard to make friends in this environment.

"I've seen you before, you know."

I was waiting at the bus stop after my last class of the day.

"I've seen you too," I said, because not only did I recognize the girl from Intro to Psychology, I often saw her on my bus, coming and going from North Point.

What she meant, though, was that she had seen me that first night in Hong Kong, when I'd wandered around in my American clothes. Her name was Au-Yeung.

"I thought you were stuck up when we first met," she later confided, "but then you let me copy your notes. I practically needed a magnifying glass!"

My written English had improved rapidly because...well, it had to. I took extensive notes in all of my classes, writing so small that not even the person sitting next to me could read them. I had developed my minuscule style back in Macau, not wanting my mother, if she happened to glance over, to see the political papers I was working on, or the Komsomol precepts I copied out in order to memorize them. *Be an entity unto yourself,* one such precept advised, *the better to help you survive if you are cut off from comrades.*

An entity unto myself. Sure, so long as my allegiance was to the Party more than to my own self-preservation!

Earlier today, in the Safeway at South Shore to buy milk and bananas, I started crying. At first I didn't know why, but then I got to the cashier's counter and looked out the window. The Alta Bates Satellite

Cancer Center was across the street. How many Fridays during the first seven months of Steve's illness did we go there to see Dr. Irving? Every Friday. Then it also became every Monday, because the blood test had to be taken within two days. Steve would get his blood drawn at the nearby lab and we'd meet with the doctor in the afternoon. We monitored the results of those blood tests the way others studied stock market ticker scrolls. WBC, but CEA in particular—we never wanted them to be high, as if we were short sellers.

During Steve's last stay in the hospital, each night as I was leaving, I would say, "Try to do a bit of walking before you go to bed, okay? It will help your circulation and keep your ankles from swelling."

"I will. Don't worry."

Some nights, he walked while I was still there, with me or his father for company—his emaciated body in the hospital gown, his eyes ringed with exhaustion, and his cheek bones protruding as he shuffled along, holding on to the intravenous apparatus with its sac of antibiotics.

What is the point, God? I thought. *Why tell him to walk, to struggle more, to keep working hard until the day he dies?* But how could I *not* tell him to walk. How could I not give him hope for improvement even on the eve of hopelessness?

I decided to write a letter to Mrs. Tang, to tell her that I wanted out of the Komsomol. I didn't give all of my reasons, but I did say that, for Chinese people, it seemed a mistake to try and minimize personal relationships and mandate compassion only for the suffering masses. China had six thousand years of history. It was a history of dynasties and communities, in which personal relationships were everything, not one shaped by the dictates of a single overarching ideology. I then reminded her of what she had said, that being a member was voluntary.

Weeks passed. Months. No word came from her or anyone else.

Still, I was paranoid. I anticipated being accosted, hustled away to an undisclosed location for interrogation or worse. Colleges like mine were strategically important places for the Communists to plant their agents, positioning them to foment and take control of student uprisings—especially in a city where China had less influence than in Macau. I had been told by my supervisor that Mao's government maintained an extensive spy network in Hong Kong. So the Komsomol was all around me, invisible. No way would I be unconditionally released, I assumed.

Probably, I would have found it easier to manage those months of suspense and uncertainty and looming dread if I hadn't felt somewhat unmoored again. My commute to and from school made college seem as provisional as the room my family rented, and it kept me from establishing disciplined study habits or, as I said, deep connections with classmates. The Komsomol had given purpose and structure to my life outside of school—over and beyond it, I should say. I didn't want to be a part of it anymore, but I did miss the positive feedback I used to get from supervisors, and I missed the clearly defined, if mostly secret, identity that being in the Komsomol gave me. After four years of having my mind and behavior molded by revolutionaries in an underground organization, I had only my own teenage philosophy and life-experience to guide me, especially since I never sought my mother's opinions on important matters, and with my father I just wasn't in the habit;

although he was with us most days now, he had been such an inconstant presence. In one sense then, Perseverance—the name I'd used when I applied to the Komsomol—was dead; in another, she was being born anew.

Despite our living situation, my mother was more lighthearted than I had ever seen her. Ngoi-Gung wasn't around to berate her nor Ngoi-Po to unfavorably compare her life to Auntie Lily's in Beverly Hills. And she was back in her natural habitat, the city where she had been a socialite before the Japanese War, and home to many of her friends from Ginling College. Socially busy, she didn't have idle hours to try and fill by nagging me, although at first she insisted I keep reporting how I spent my allowance.

"You don't need to know that, if I understand what the allowance is supposed to cover and what it isn't," I said.

My father agreed and the matter was dropped.

One would think that with my mother no longer plaguing me, I too would be more lighthearted, or at least wouldn't slam my fist through glass doors and otherwise act out. But I kept erupting into anger over what should have been slight annoyances, if that. Was it hormones? My migraines were less frequent, but my periods were still lasting eight to ten days, and PMS came with fainting spells, nausea, and vomiting along with the typical cramps. Or did I act out because I hadn't dared when the duster was a threat, and I was now testing limits? Maybe it was a bit of both. But it always came as a surprise—the hot, swelling rage that overwhelmed me. I threw things at walls, and one lunchtime, because no beef was on offer, I upended the table, sending everything spilling and clattering to the floor. My mother called for Ah Ying to clean it up.

I occasionally think I should stop all of this, that shuffling through memories is no way to grieve. Then I wonder if the loss of my husband has made me aware of a lifetime of losses. Well, there have been gains too, both hard-won and serendipitous, but...who am I, after all? People like me are a dime a dozen. Might *that* somehow be a reason to continue?

"Free associate," therapists like to tell patients. But get too carried away, they don't say, and you could end up in treatment for decades, if not the rest of your life.

There is an advantage to being crazy, with grief or otherwise: you're accepted by mental health professionals.

Before my first semester was over, it became clear that my grandparents would have to come and live with us in Hong Kong. None of the maids hired to look after them lasted long, unable or unwilling to tolerate Ngoi-Gung's abuse, and my mother often traveled to Macau to sort out their domestic situation.

So again she hunted for a suitable flat and this time had better luck, finding a three-bedroom overlooking the water on the North Point docks. It featured a full bath, and a small toilet on the balcony for Ah Ying and the new maid. My parents lived in the front room, my grandparents in the middle one. I had a tiny space in back next to the kitchen, and the maids slept on a bunkbed in a storage alcove between the two main bedrooms.

For a while my grandparents were as happy as they were ever going to get, my grandfather praising the sea breeze and my grandmother liking the size of their room and the view. But it was a short while.

"Are you trying to kill me or are you just stupid?" Ngoi-Gung would bark at whoever he heard tramping near. "I'll catch pneumonia! Close the windows!"

Trying to get him to behave, my grandmother would threaten divorce, then go around making amends, but as she shuffled morosely past me, I sometimes heard her mumble: Ngoi-Gung would have no cause for grievous outbursts in Beverly Hills.

It was hardly a secret that my father wasn't respected by his in-laws, that they believed he should have provided a better life for their daughter. He could have said the same to them, I thought, but he remained cordial and never reminded them that without him they would be homeless.

"Where is that girl?" my grandfather impatiently called one morning.

"Here," I said, stepping from my room.

"Come and sit down." He felt his way toward the kitchen, the dining table. "You have to eat a good breakfast."

His insistence was exactly like Luther Chang's years before. Eggs. Ham. Buttered toast or congee. Milk tea. I didn't like to eat so much first thing in the day.

"He just wants what he thinks is best for his grandchild," my mother whispered, but not softly enough.

"*She's* not my grandchild!" Grandpa Ho sneered.

I didn't understand, not right away, and my mother didn't push back. She didn't say, *Of course she's your granddaughter, and Bentham is your grandson*, because she knew: we were *ngoi*, his daughter's children; legitimate grandchildren, heirs, came from sons.

"You, sit and eat," he commanded every morning.

I never argued and finished whatever Ah Ying put in front of me while Grandpa Ho sat there, listening with a blind man's ears. What did he care if I had a "good breakfast," non-grandchild that I was? I despised him, and I doubt I would have been forgiving if I'd thought of it—how his insistence might have grown out of his early years as a poor boy in Hawaii, when he used to make a single egg last him a week so that his younger siblings had enough to eat. No, I had no head for extenuating circumstances, for anything that could make me sympathetic toward him. I was filled with mute hatred, hearing that old man's vigilant breath as I pushed ham and toast into my mouth and then, around the corner from our building, on my way to school, forced myself to vomit.

I'm down to ninety-four pounds. I need to call my doctor's office and ask what happened to the referrals for an abdominal ultrasound and colonoscopy.

How odd life is, unpredictable and relentless: Steve suffered and died; I suffer and days and nights lie ahead of me.

We visited Bonita Cove yesterday—my daughters, Napoleon and I. We brought two bouquets of tulips and roses and baby's breath, one from me and the other from the girls. It was a windy afternoon, and when we threw our flowers into the water, the high, breaking waves carried some of them back to shore. My elder daughter and I waded into the surf, tossed them seaward again and again.

In the evening, her boyfriend met us at the house. I showed him where Steve kept his best clothes—the Burberry hats and coats, the Ralph Lauren suits, the Hickey Freeman blazers, the Cable Car pants, everything he'd bought on sale but rarely wore.

"Please," I said, "you can have whatever you like that fits you."

Not easy words for me. It is taking a long time to part with Steve's things. I used to complain that the only imperfection in our house was its lack of closet space, little thinking that one day it would be more than sufficient.

Educated and intelligent as my father was, he never had good luck or timing in his career. A frost—a fluke weather event in subtropical Kowloon—destroyed his papaya crop, and with his partner unwilling to invest further, he had to find a job. An ideal opening presented itself: a government position managing one of the Agricultural Department's farms. It offered good pay and benefits. It was the sort of position he could keep for the rest of his working days, which would comfortably provide for him in retirement.

"I don't want it," he said.

But wasn't it his dream job? He could lead by example and bring local farming into the twentieth century, helping improve farmers' lives, increasing their efficiency and productivity, feeding more people.

"I don't want to be forever kicked in the ass by the English," he said, meaning that he refused to work for the colonial government.

"But if you're so against serving the British, why don't you return to China?" I asked.

"Please," my mother cut in, "keep your voices down. The neighbors will hear you fighting."

"So what?"

"We're not fighting. We're *discussing*," I said and turned to my father, wondering if he was a hypocrite, progressive in thought but unwilling to subject himself to a spartan existence on the mainland for his espoused cause. "Communists or not, the poor conditions of peasant farmers are the same and you can help them."

He shook his head. "Bentham could be purged for having a British official as a father."

He might have had a point—my brother was near the end of his medical training in Beijing—but it was not well taken by me or my mother. A high-level government job would have significantly improved our lives, both economically and socially, to the point where even my grandparents would have been forced to respect my father as a provider. Besides, he could have accepted what power was given him by the colonizers and used it to undermine them.

"Allison Liu has a son on the mainland, doesn't she?" I asked my mother, referring to a friend of hers.

For a woman who liked to adamantly wield rattan dusters, she was being oddly meek. "Yes," she answered.

"And her husband has his ass kicked constantly by the British to win government contracts and they've gotten rich and the Chinese don't concern themselves with their son," I said.

Yes, she said, as far as she knew, this was true. But my father refused to change his mind.

It was a rare moment of unity: my mother and I both thought he was making a big mistake. But where I tried to reason with him, she started crying. Which irritated me because I thought it weak, unintelligent. What did crying like that ever get anyone? It wasn't a cathartic cry. It was an admission of helplessness, of subordination—to people and circumstances. It was needless surrender.

My father found a job as superintendent of a Christian orphanage.

The second of three sons, my father was still a baby when Grandpa Taam left his village in Guangdong and traveled to Canton, where he became a carpenter's apprentice. Once he had more than learned the craft, he sent for his wife and children. Natural talent added to his carpentry skills and he found steady work, eventually expanding into the general construction business. Grandpa Taam helped build the customs house and post office, and after he became an evangelist in his fifties, he built all of the Presbyterian churches in the capital.

My father grew up amid the family's increasing prosperity and studied zoology at Nanjing University, which he claimed was a way to ease into the medical field. Did he sincerely believe this or was it his way of indirectly, gradually distancing himself from Grandpa Taam's ambitions for him? Yer-Yer, as my daughters and I called my paternal grandfather, wanted his three sons to be doctors. China was poor in healthcare, he said. He would send them to America for graduate school, they would get their medical degrees, and return to help the mainland. But after my parents met at an intercollegiate event, my dad went on a summer bike trip to a village with his eventual brothers-in-law, where he saw how poor the farmers were.

"Some families had to share a single pair of pants," he told me years later. "Today, the father goes to the market, he wears the pants. Tomorrow, a son has to run an errand, he wears the pants. The next day…"

On that bike trip, he decided a career in agriculture could be more impactful than one in medicine, enabling him to help entire rural populations instead of individual patients. So when he left for Cornell, it wasn't to study medicine. Was Grandpa Taam disappointed? Not enough to stop him. It wasn't the first time Yer-Yer's plans for a son had been thwarted. His eldest studied political science at Stanford and afterward became the first Chinese to graduate from the New York Police Academy. He returned to China for several years, working in a high-level government job about which I know little—he had aspirations to establish a kind of CIA— but during the second Japanese War, he again left for America. He married a UC Berkeley graduate who opened a gift shop in San Francisco, and he spent the rest of his life puttering about there, failing to make himself important to the local tongs.

Uncle Chung, my dad's younger brother, finally fulfilled Yer-Yer's wishes—mostly. He earned his medical degree from Johns Hopkins and became an orthopedic surgeon, but prevented from returning to China because of World War II, he settled in Fresno.

If no one's come looking for almost a year, I reasoned, *they must have decided to let me go*. I suppose it happened with a lot of young people: the Komsomol used us for as long as they could; some became full-fledged members of the Communist Party, many—as young people do—lost interest and moved on. Of course, I had no idea that my time in the organization would influence my career choice and resound through the rest of my life. And I *am* glad that I was active during the early years of Mao's rise, when comrades from the Chairman himself down to the most humble were, so I believe, pure in their purpose to eradicate poverty and corruption and—in contrast to a Nationalist government bereft of statesmanship, plagued by graft, and heavily influenced by the West—to establish the country's self-sufficiency. The trouble with Chinese Communist Party policies didn't start until the 1960s, when relations with the USSR began to fray and after the Great Leap Forward, a campaign intended to turn China into an industrialized nation, had brought famine to millions and proved a miracle of economic mismanagement. But as I say, that was after my time. One can read about these things online or in textbooks, and my life is not a textbook.

Free of the Komsomol, I stopped fearfully glancing over my shoulder for would-be abductors; as much as I was constitutionally able, I let myself relax. *I've come into my own*, I thought. *The days of needing to attach myself to someone or something—Chan Pei, Mrs. Tang, a political organization—are over.* But then came Alex Liu and it seemed that determination wasn't necessarily mine to make.

The younger son of Allison, my mother's friend, Alex was a junior at Hong Kong University, pursuing a degree in engineering. At first we saw each other only during family gatherings. He was outgoing, good-natured, and handsome in a Gregory Peck sort of way, with a square jaw, aquiline nose, distinguished eyebrows, and piercing gaze. Most importantly, he had a strong hairline and didn't wear glasses. I refused to date anyone bespectacled or bald. Silly, but that's how I was.

"What's your favorite color?" I asked him.

Half-joking, he said he was too busy studying to have one.

"That's too bad. I can't date anybody who doesn't like the color blue."

"Blue!" He grinned. "My favorite color is blue!"

He liked that I had definite if sometimes peculiar ideas and tended to express them. He liked that I made all of the decisions about what movies we went to and where we ate. Our parents didn't push us to be together or in any way interfere, although we both knew they would be pleased if we married. And Alex, who spent so much of his time with books, was as inclined as his mother toward engagement. Every other aspect of his future was already decided. His father—an engineer and successful businessman—had plans for him to inherit the family's construction company, since his older brother had been lost to the Communists. Alex was to earn his undergraduate degree, go abroad to Oxford for his master's, resettle in Hong Kong, and work at his father's company until it became his own. Having such an educated, wealthy man for a husband, my life would be established on a high footing. What more could a young bourgeois woman in 1950s Hong Kong ask for?

With the university still under construction my sophomore year, the quarters for kitchen staff were being used as an interim girls' dorm. About fifty of us were housed there. I shared a room with six others, including Au-Yeung and a girl named Bess, who was studying Business Administration and whom I had likewise met on my commutes to and from the campus. Bess's bed was attached to mine at one end. Au-Yeung's was only about two feet away. As small and crowded as our room was, I felt like a sparrow finally free of my cage; it was my first time living away from my family.

Because of my leaky heart valve, I had to take dance instruction instead of P.E., which was supposed to be less physically stressful, and I convinced Au-Yeung and Bess to take it with me. The instructor was the university president's wife—a Ginling alum and a good friend of my mother's. She also happened to be something of a drill sergeant. A petite, solid woman with a commanding voice, she started every class without preliminaries, marching in and yelling, "Jump, step-step, skip, step-step!" or some such variation. We would hurry to our assigned positions and try to keep up with her shouted instructions. At least once, she saw us laughing.

"What's so funny?"

"I'm just happy to be dancing," I lied.

Out of breath after class, I said to my friends, "Jump-Step-Step is going to kill me." And that's how she got her nickname: Jump-Step-Step.

"I wonder if she's like that with her husband," Bess said, and we cracked up, picturing—or trying not to—Jump-Step-Step in a private moment with the university president.

I was the only student from Macau left; of the four boys who'd come to college with me, two dropped out and the others had gone overseas to study. I chose to major in Language and Literature, intending to be a journalist and eventually the editor of a newspaper. I made this decision without consulting my parents and they never questioned me about it, possibly because I was a good student. I was finding it easy to meet or exceed my professors' expectations, which didn't always involve academic work. The room in which I had English Conversation was—as with so many others—inevitably hot and humid. The missionary lady who taught the class used to open the window first thing. I doubted this was a smart move, since outside *was* Hong Kong, which is another way of saying "hot and humid and crazy with insects." Still, when I noticed her routine, I started opening the window for her as soon as she walked in.

"And you think that's why you got the only A+ in the class?" Au-Yeung asked.

"I'm sure of it."

We were in the middle of our meal-making ritual—me, Au-Yeung, and Bess. We had formed our own sorority, BCF, which stood for Bread, Cans, and Friendship. Why this name? Because we were so busy with our studies, and because the food in the cafeteria was getting worse as more students enrolled at Chung Chi, we often bought bread and canned goods and made sandwiches and other quick meals for ourselves in our room.

"I don't know," Bess said, working the can opener. "You weren't *that* bad at conversation."

Actually, I had been pretty good because I never cared if I made mistakes.

"Not bad isn't A+ level, though, is it?" I said.

Being unafraid to make mistakes, I believed, was a distinctly American mindset: as long as one tried, it didn't matter how good one really was. In Chinese culture, one tries to never make mistakes.

Alex and I were supposed to be going steady and we were constantly in touch, but because we didn't see each other often, we agreed that we could date other people so long as we were honest and forthcoming about it. I'm pretty sure he wasn't interested in dating, for the same reason that I myself didn't see a lot of him; he was intensely preparing for Oxford in the coming fall. He probably went along with the dating idea only to please me, not believing I would explore options. He was right; I didn't. Why would I, when he could provide a better future than any other boy I knew—an upper-class life of luxury and influence, with the freedom to travel to faraway places for vacations? Attachment to him was easy and comfortable. He was nearby but not smothering; as his girlfriend, I had space and security.

The freedom and means to travel to faraway places for vacations: I didn't equate this with having a magic carpet. The carpet I had been dreaming about for years wasn't for little excursions, fleeting distractions; it would deliver me to my destiny.

Bess and I were frequently the talk of boys, I was told at a college reunion in America long after the fact. Evidently, they used to argue about which of us was prettier.

Bess—quick to blush, shy, with a charming smile—never dated. The boys who approached her tended to be less academic; they were more the flamboyant, playboy type, so she was cautious about responding to them.

Three boys in particular—I should call them young men—were interested in me. The most earnest was Kao, a chemistry major along with Au-Yeung, an honor student who, without family support, had not only managed his path through college but had secured a scholarship for graduate study at the University of Virginia. Au-Yeung informed him that I had a boyfriend, but he remained undeterred. He was confident about his future and the girl he wanted. I admired his tenacity but wasn't interested in more than friendship.

In China, courtship is more subtle than in the United States. One doesn't come right out and tell people, *I do not like you, sorry.* One suggests it indirectly, in as polite a way as possible—through friends or modest, distancing behavior. Since it is considered an honor to be admired, you do not bluntly brush aside such things. Back then, among my peer group at least, openly expressive passion was discouraged by society and so love was romanticized; I, and most other girls, became screens on which admirers projected their idealized love. For example, Kao. He might have thought, *I'm in love with this girl, and although she's with someone else, that's likely because of her parents or family situation. Fate will bring us together. I must not give up.*

I felt bad for Au-Yeung because no young men were interested in her. She was terribly shy around them, but studying organic chemistry didn't help; it was considered a masculine field.

"What about boys in your major?" I asked.

"All they ever talk to me about is *chemistry!*" she said.

Long before, despite Big Sis's physical advances and Tsang Shuet King confessing her love in middle school, I had come to believe that I wasn't very likable. But there I was, in college with friends and admirers and a boyfriend, so I assumed that I must have been wrong. The assumption is still with me and has helped me learn to love myself. I want to be clear: to this day, I cannot see anything in myself to love, but I feel love from others and it reverberates. If people love me, there must be something lovable in me, so why can't I love myself?

I went home on weekends. Usually, it was late morning by the time I reached downtown Hong Kong, where my mother would be waiting at the ferry. We'd spend a couple of hours shopping for clothes, then stop for lunch on our way to the flat. She would talk about her social life and ask after Alex, but not too eagerly, speculating as to which of my new outfits might please him best. She never asked how I liked school, which professors were my favorite, or if I had any friends besides Au-Yeung and Bess. I kept my conversation to the superficial, on the concrete here and now of our activities, whether browsing in a shop or ordering food. But I suppose it was good for us to just exist in each other's company. Those afternoons must have been a reprieve for her, different than what her friends could provide because I was her daughter. They allowed her an illusion of family-togetherness to temper the reality of life at home with her father, who stewed in darkness and rage during his waking hours, listening to the BBC and railing at everyone.

I had for the most part been spared from Ngoi-Gung's worst behaviors, but that began to change.

"Would you like me to get your coffee for you?" I asked at breakfast one morning, trying to be helpful.

I set the cup before him and dropped in his usual single cube of sugar. After helping the sugar dissolve with a spoon, he lifted the cup to his lips.

"It's too sweet. You put in too much sugar."

"I put in the amount you like—one cube."

"No, you didn't! I think I know the taste of my coffee! You put in too much!"

"Ngoi-Gung, I—"

"Liar!" he flared at me. "LIAR!"

Being accused of things I didn't do enraged me. It still does, and the therapist in me wonders if my anger derives from when my mother beat me for not admitting to misbehavior or petty dishonesty of which I was innocent. Whatever the case, by my teenage years I had developed an acute sense of injustice at being unfairly accused, so being presumed guilty of lying by a man who rejected me and Bentham as his legitimate grandchildren caused me to snap.

"You're an ungrateful old fool!" I yelled.

Ngoi-Gung picked up his breakfast knife, pointed it in my direction. "I'll kill you! You're dead, swine!"

I grabbed the knife from him, threw it aside, and told him to stop his stupidity and rudeness or I would call the police and he'd be taken away to an insane asylum. Overhearing this, my father came out of his room and slapped me—the only time in my life he laid a hand on me.

"Stop being disrespectful."

I stomped to my room, determined to sever my relationship with Grandpa Ho. I didn't care what was culturally expected—deference to my elders, obedience. I didn't care what others would say or think. I wanted to live in relative peace and I'd had enough nonsense from this octogenarian who had made life at home miserable since I was nine, with the maids and Ngoi-Po crying and apologizing, my mother ever failing to please him, and my father staying out as often as he could to avoid hearing an old man yell and complain.

"I'm never going to talk to him again," I swore to my mother. "I won't have anything to do with him for as long as he lives."

She begged me to change my mind. That was a first—my mother tearfully appealing to me, my so-called better nature. I wished I could have satisfied her, but no, not in this instance. I was angry at her too, for neglecting our family's comfort in favor of caring for her parents, and I privately vowed that when I was older, I wouldn't subject my own children to living in a three-generation household.

"I can promise you one thing," I told her. "Even though I'll have nothing to do with Ngoi-Gung, I will never cause a scene and embarrass you in front of your friends. And I'll behave normally to Ngoi-Po. But the best thing the two of you can do is ignore him. Don't give him the interaction that leads to his raving."

From then on, as I came and went from the flat, I paid no attention to my grandfather—not greeting him or saying hello, not acknowledging his presence in a room or responding if he tried to provoke me. He eventually tried to be nice and engage me in conversation and I was tempted to relent, but I reminded myself: paranoid and senile as he was, he would be pleasant for a little while and revert to his old ways, which he couldn't help. So I stayed strong, and what went on between him and the rest of the family became none of my business. I was oblivious. Even now I'm amazed at the degree of my detachment. But my life has turned out to be like a bureau with many drawers: some drawers I open regularly; others I keep closed for long stretches of time, not wanting to consider what's inside; yet others, once closed, have never been reopened and I've forgotten what they hold. This bureau appears organized, as such furnishings tend to do, with each drawer situated in a particular way to all the others. But it's becoming unwieldy; I add more drawers to it every year, not knowing which, once I close them, will never again be opened.

As to my non-engagement with my grandfather, Ngoi-Po expressed no direct opinion. Instead, she encouraged me more emphatically to work hard, urging—as I imagine she formerly urged my mother and her sisters, not wanting them to end up like her—that I prioritize my education.

"Study well," she said. "Pay attention and be independent."

Gung-Gung and Po-Po: my father's parents, Grandpa and Grandma Taam.

Ngoi-Gung's first dental office in Nanjing, circa 1907. My grandfather, cane in hand, is looking directly at the camera.

Ngoi-Gung and Ngoi-Po (on the right) in Honolulu circa 1905, posing with the family of Dr. Li, who arranged their marriage. My mom is in Ngoi-Po's lap. Auntie Lily sits in front of her.

Ngoi-Gung and Ngoi-Po's Nanjing mansion, built thanks to Grandpa's successful dental practice.

My parents, Harry and Ivy, on their wedding day, 1930, in San Diego, where Uncle Albert and Auntie Lily lived before moving to Beverly Hills.

Another from my parents' wedding in San Diego, the guests a mixture of East and West. Auntie Lily, next to my father, is holding her first child (Alberta).

My brother Bentham on a Hong Kong rooftop, late 1930s.

Bentham and I in Hong Kong, before our family fled into the interior to escape the Japanese.

A formal portrait of my parents, around the time of their wedding.

The Ho family (l. to r.): my mom and Bentham, Auntie Doris, Ngoi-Po, Uncle Ernest, Alberta (Uncle Albert and Auntie Lily's firstborn), Uncle Guy, Ngoi-Gung, Uncle David, Auntie Lily with Liliane on her lap.

My mom and Bentham, 1930s.

My mother, 1940.

Auntie Amy, a pathologist and one of my first role models, outside our cottage in Macau.

Ah Ying (right), my proletariat comrade whom I taught to read and write when I was in the Komsomol, worked years for my family.

My parents and my godfather (right).

My father in Nanjing. He might have been a university student at the time.

The Taam brothers (l. to r.): Dad, Uncle Chung, Uncle Wu. All three attended graduate school in the States, but only my father used a western name.

Uncle Albert, Auntie Lily, and their kids in the backyard of their Beverly Hills home, 1950.

Steve and his mother Mary in Canton, before they came to America.

Uncle Albert with his arm around me at his mother's ninetieth birthday party.

Top row (l to r): Uncle Ernest, my godfather, Dad, Bentham, Auntie Amy.
Bottom row (l to r): Mom, Ngoi-Po, me, Ngoi-Gung, Auntie Lily.

Aboard a steamship, seeing Auntie Lily off after a visit, 1950s.

Dressed in a feminine style to please my mother, a ribbon in my hair, for a portrait with Bentham.

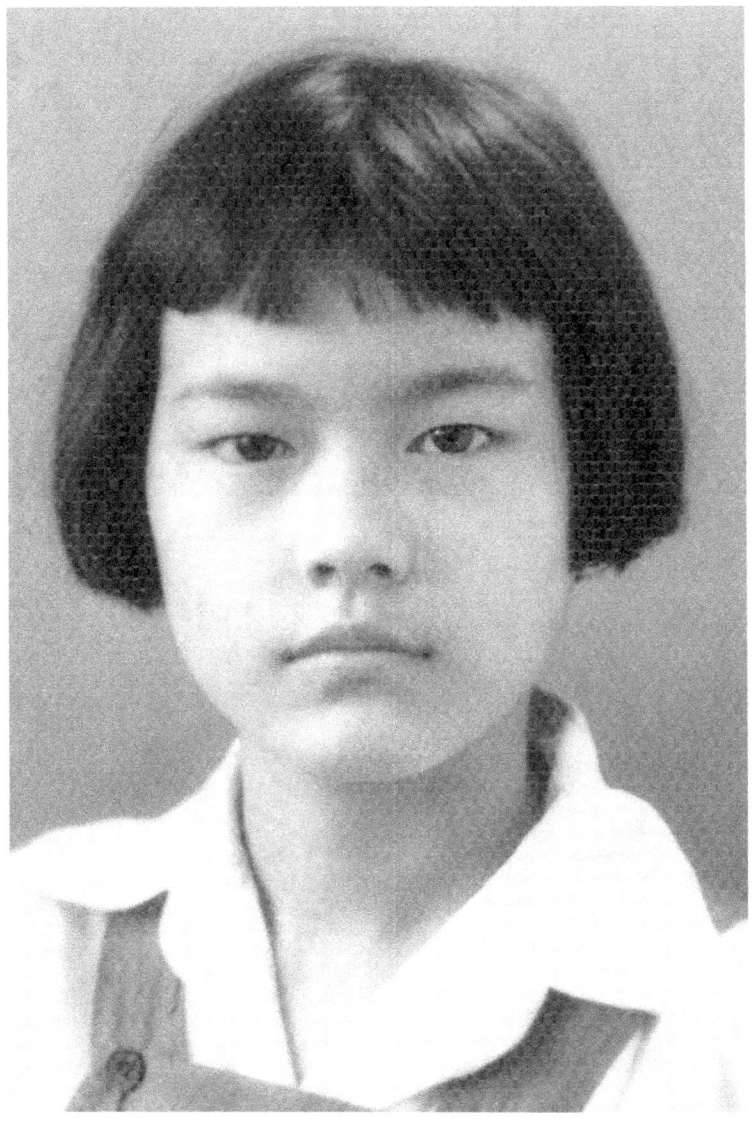

Just after my first act of rebellion: getting my hair cut in the style of Joan of Arc.

Ngoi-Po and Ngoi-Gung.

My brother, Mom, and I on the rooftop of Auntie Fong's apartment in Canton, where I engaged in the un-girly activity of flying kites.

With Uncle Ernest's wife, who later took her own life.

My parents and I at my graduation from Chung Chi College, Hong Kong.

My valedictory speech at graduation. I don't look half as nervous as I felt.

One of the receptions after Steve and I married, hosted by his parents: a traditional Chinese banquet.

Steve and I at our wedding in 1962, with Auntie Lily and Uncle Albert seated next to Steve.

Steve's parents, Harold and Mary, with our daughters, late 1960s.

Steve as a fresh graduate from Officers Candidate School in Rhode Island, May 1965.

The two of us, celebrating his accomplishment. I'm pregnant with my first child.

Steve at Treasure Island, San Francisco Bay.

My daughters, early 1970s.

A Hong Kong shantytown, where I did my first fieldwork.

On a visit to a Hong Kong shantytown.

The shantytowns, filled with refugees from the Communist mainland, were on hillsides. The traditional *cheongsam* I wore was less than ideal for the long hikes to visit them!

Giving a speech at a fundraiser for the Family Outreach Program, Oakland 1973.

7

MY STEP-GRANDMOTHER IN CANTON and Auntie Amy were the only family members in touch with Bentham—Amy because she lived in Peking; Po-Po because she was paying for my brother's education, which, since he didn't come from proletariat stock, wasn't being subsidized by Mao's government. My parents, as unrepentant bourgeoisie, weren't allowed to contact him or vice versa, and so the only news we received came through Po-Po's correspondence.

"Why didn't you have more children?" I asked my mother, watching her greedy eyes track back and forth, taking in one of those newsy letters.

I hadn't planned on asking, the words just came out. I'd never asked her a personal question before, but the way she was devouring that letter...

If she'd had more sons, would she have been less pained by Bentham's absence, his having decided his future for himself at seventeen—a future that didn't include us? It was the norm for Chinese families to consist of five or six kids. I certainly wouldn't have minded growing up with a younger brother to play with and care for, or a slightly older sister who could have acted as a mother-substitute.

She didn't answer my question. I asked again. Why didn't she have more children?

"Poor health," she answered without looking up. I waited until she finished reading to hear more. "Your brother was premature and my pregnancy with you was complicated. I weighed eighty pounds when you were born."

That was when I first remembered—my father, in Canton, casually telling me that Maa-Mi was in the hospital, offering no further details, and the maids later whispering of abortion.

I had my first taste of alcohol at about the age of three. Before the Japanese War, when we lived on Prince Edward Road in Kowloon, my father used to carry me around during parties, giving me sips of his drinks. By the time I was four, we were in Guilin, displaced by the violence of the Japanese, and he often sent me out to buy Camel cigarettes two blocks from our house. He was a chain-smoker, adept at blowing smoke rings, which fascinated me. I never dared take a cigarette from a new pack. Instead, I started picking up his smoldering butts and taught myself to smoke, and I went from choking and coughing to being able to form loose, quickly disintegrating circle-like clouds.

At Chung Chi I was a bit of an instigator, a not-always-great influence on others. I taught Au-Yeung and Bess to drink and smoke. I had befriended the groundskeeper who lived in the old villa on campus, and she let me have small gatherings there. No boys were ever invited. I didn't think them capable of keeping the secret and we would be expelled if word got out. So it was just us girls, drinking and smoking. I doubt any of us really enjoyed these presumably adult activities; by doing them, we were announcing to ourselves that we were in fact no longer girls but young women. We played poker too, which I had taught to everyone, having learned from watching my mother and her friends, whom she had taught. Unlike most Chinese women throughout the ages, my mother didn't care for mahjong.

"Please don't come," Bess said.

"You're distracting," Au-Yeung explained.

It was exam time and they were going to the library to study.

Lucky for them, I found the library too confining. After twenty or thirty minutes of concentration, I would need to get up for a drink of water or a trip to the bathroom to wash my face or I'd want to chat, whatever. I absorbed class material better by talking to people about it. None of which helped my friends' study habits, apparently, and off to the library they would go while I stayed in the dorm and "studied" with the RA, a widow in her fifties who frequently made soup for us. She also read palms and told fortunes.

"You will be married to a government official," she informed me. "You won't be rich but will live comfortably. You will have three children."

In the end, she wasn't totally wrong about the children. I had three pregnancies, one of them ending in a miscarriage.

"Despite being an honor student," she said, "and strong-minded, you will not have much success in your own career, but you will be your husband's confidante and adviser, invaluable in helping him achieve his professional goals."

What?! I thought. *I have big dreams, bigger than the Panavision screens in the movie theaters!* Maybe I still couldn't have told her or anyone else precisely what those big dreams were, but I could say what they weren't—being a mere adjunct to a man.

In 1957, my mother was allowed to visit Bentham in Beijing. Alex's older brother was graduating from medical school. Mrs. Liu, whose husband had been made a Justice of the Peace by the British, was granted permission to attend the ceremony—part of a propaganda campaign to prove that Mao's government was friendly to Britain and the people of Hong Kong. She invited my mother along as her companion. They were gone for ten days.

"He's working as a surgeon in Beijing Hospital," my mother reported on her return; also, that most of Bentham's wardrobe consisted of what he'd brought with him from Canton after his last year of high school, and much of it was ragged and had been repeatedly mended. Since buying him new clothes was bourgeois and therefore out of the question, she herself had tried to further mend his wardrobe, but he'd stopped her.

"If I can sew up people's stomachs, I can certainly mend my own clothes," he had said, which became something she chucklingly recalled to help ease the pain of having lost her son to the struggling new country.

Another prophecy my RA wasn't wrong about: me being Steve's adviser. I realize that it's not as unusual as it once was for wives to be sounding boards for their husbands, though I don't like referring to us as *boards*, turning wives into *things*. But speaking of…

Steve worked most of his professional life for the San Francisco Board of Education, starting as a Planner and rising to Director of School Maintenance. So my husband *was* a government official. Driven as he was, he always wanted to strategize with me about office politics—the best way of impressing his bosses, getting projects approved, maneuvering nimbly upward in that bureaucratic tangle. He knew that my work was important to me, but he never asked about it, probably assuming I was efficient and in control. There were times at the end of a day, however, when I was ready to collapse, when I felt weak and helpless and wanted to *receive*, not *give*, but—

"What do you think...?" he would begin, and I'd fall into the role of listener and adviser, which left little room or inclination for me to try and strategize with him about *my* work.

Success. Of course there are many ways to define it—material wealth, one's beneficial influence or impact on others, personal happiness and fulfillment. When my RA said that I wouldn't have much success in my career, how was she defining it?

The summer after my sophomore year, Alex and I lost our virginity to each other. With both of our mothers in Beijing, my dad spending weeknights at the orphanage, and Alex's father in England on a business trip, the opportunities were abundant. We didn't plan on doing it, nor was it an explosive moment of lust. Our relationship wasn't terribly romantic or obsessive. It's hard to describe, really. We had important things in common: as far as education went, our family backgrounds were similar; our older brothers had been fleeting figures in our lives and we had each grown up like an only child; and we both felt the pressure exerted by our families and our culture to find a spouse, sooner rather than later, and have children. We had heard so many stories about love—how the passionate sort never lasted and caused regret and misery, but a more reserved affection, cultivated over time, through a practical partnership founded upon mutual respect and clearly defined roles, *that* was real-world love, appropriate for responsible adults.

With Alex and me, there was definitely some heat and desire, but we were driven more by instinct, curiosity, and a companionship that had developed as we blossomed into adults. The sex just sort of happened—at his family's Repulse Bay beach house a few days into our mothers' trip. We got in a lot of practice before they came back, and more afterward, and we practiced right up until Alex left for Oxford in August, promising to write and call.

An adjunct. Wasn't that what I'd be with Alex? We would have wealth and comfort, yes, but he'd be like his father, working all the time, busy with local politics. And as a prominent citizen's wife, I would have countless social obligations, at which I'd act as his de facto representative, just as Mrs. Liu did for her husband—hosting events, sitting on boards of charitable organizations, cutting red ribbons at openings. Did I want a marriage shaped by so much absence, my husband's attention constantly directed elsewhere? Hadn't I, with those I should have been closest to, already experienced enough of such absences?

I found myself praying, *Please, God, so that the man who loves me can be with me all the time, maybe it would be best if he's unemployed.*

This morning, I attended a Second Cycle of Bereavement Group meeting. I hadn't been in months. There were eight of us, all women. Four of them were first-timers: two had lost their husbands; the others, their fathers. The husbands, before they died, had meticulously detailed everything to their wives, leaving pages of instructions about what to do with their investments and other business concerns. Steve had done nothing of the kind, knowing that I could handle such things because we were equal partners in household finances and all investments had been thoroughly discussed between us. But since when does a woman's knowledge keep her from an earful of mansplaining? Steve not writing out instructions for me: this was his refusal to give up.

Nance, the therapist who runs Second Cycle, encouraged the more experienced among us to participate. But everything seemed irrelevant to me: illness, dying, death, sorrow, grief, fear. I kept silent.

"You look angry," Lu said.

"I don't feel she's angry," Evelyn, who was next to me, said.

"I'm just tired," I said.

"You look tired," Nance said.

Walking to my car after the meeting, I stopped to watch a plane cross the sky. Then another, traveling in a different direction. How I wished that I could be a plane with a charted course, knowing where and when I would land, and making my way confidently across the vast, empty distance above the clouds.

Spring, insensitive to how I feel, has arrived. Spring, with all its freshness and vitality and new growth. Outside, the trees with their bright green leaves are quiet in the windless afternoon, as if standing there, listening. But to what? To whom?

"You're planning to major in literature?" the guidance counselor asked at the beginning of my junior year.

"I am," I said. "I would like to be a journalist, possibly a newspaper editor."

"The most likely career for you won't be in journalism. It will be as a teacher."

Why? Because I was female? I had no interest in becoming a teacher. The counselor might have been wrong, and *most likely* didn't mean I *definitely* wouldn't become a journalist, but did I want to make things harder for myself? Should I switch majors? To what?

Bess told me about a new department centered on social work and religious education.

"Religious education sounds a lot like teaching," I said.

Despite having gone to Christian schools my entire life, I had as little interest in organized religion as I did in pedagogy. I was—and remain—more of a spiritualist, which I think allows for less hypocrisy. I'm willing to grant that all or most religions meant well in their original intent, but what does that matter since time and again they're corrupted in practice by the individuals propagating them?

The Department of Social Work had been established in response to the enormous influx of refugees from the mainland. Squatters by the thousands were scattered on every once-vacant hillside, living in shelters made of flimsy boards and tin sheets. Every typhoon season, these hovels—the crowded, dirty, poverty-worn encampments—got washed away in landslides and floods. The British government was mobilizing funds to accommodate the refugees with nominally better housing, but "resettlements" couldn't be built fast enough and supply was unlikely to ever keep up with demand. The Red Cross worked tirelessly to distribute food, and an entire industry was forming to try and care for these people. Good jobs existed for those who were qualified.

Can I still be committed to helping the sick and suffering, the poor and oppressed? I had asked when I quit the Komsomol.

If it was how I made my living—yes, I could.

At the end of the first semester, I met the head of the new department, a Chinese woman with an MSW from Cambridge.

"I'm thinking of switching majors to social work," I said.

She looked over my transcript and told me that, since I had focused mostly on electives and literature, I would need to make up a lot of credits in order to graduate with my class.

"Plus, there's fieldwork."

It sounded daunting, and—fieldwork?—I didn't fully understand the commitment I was making. The poor and oppressed. The suffering and the sick. I could say these words, but they were still more abstractions than otherwise. Well, not abstractions. I had lived with war. What was abstract, vague, was what one could actually do, beyond sloganeering and talking philosophically in cemeteries, to lessen poverty, oppression, suffering, and sickness in the long term. I was clueless, but I didn't doubt that a degree in social work would provide a good foundation for any community or charitable initiatives I might undertake as Alex's wife.

"Lots of my mom's friends who studied abroad have MSWs," he said in one of our weekly calls, referring to the wives of important businessmen and politicians.

I changed majors, and for the first time in college, I had to apply myself. I attended classes on Saturday mornings at the

YWCA, as well as my regular classes during the week. I can't say that the academic studies—the history of social work, of welfare and poor houses—did much for my understanding of what I'd taken on, but that was about to change with the start of my duties in the field. It was just as well that Alex didn't come home for Christmas break.

Why was a minor in religious education required for a social work degree? Obvious answer: imperialism. Social workers toil among the needy and vulnerable—those who, desperate for a literal lifeline and hope for a future, are often the most ripe for religious indoctrination. And Chung Chi was missionary to its core. I took classes with names like Christianity and Science, Christianity and History, Christianity and Modern Life. And I began to argue with my professors.

"I don't think there's a God like the one you describe," I said to Mrs. Finske, a minister from Pennsylvania. "Or a God like the ones described in any other religion I know. My God, the one I pray to, is a general spiritual force, an energy."

As with so many professors at Chung Chi, Mrs. Finske was used to teaching in seminaries or graduate schools in America, not in rooms full of novice Chinese students possessing varying degrees of English proficiency. She gave us an assignment one time: we had a month to hand in a comparative study of the Old and New Testaments. She must have said more in terms of guidelines and scope, but whatever she told us, it wasn't enough. The topic was vast and none of us had read both the Old and New Testaments. We had only the notes we'd taken from her fast-talking lectures to go by, and no one—myself included—was sure they understood the material.

"Could we have more time?" I asked Mrs. Finske. "We're not clear on what's being asked of us because we've had trouble with the recent lessons. If you could help us understand better before we start writing our papers—"

"A month is more than enough time," she said. "If you've been attentive in class, you shouldn't have any problem comprehending the material."

Nobody was close to finishing the assignment after three weeks. The more diligent students had at most a few paragraphs, with doubtful attempts at more that petered out into blank pages. I had decided to write absolutely nothing, which reflected what I thought I knew about the subject.

"You're not going to hand in *anything*?" my classmates asked.

"I'm not, no."

One by one, discussing it among themselves, my classmates decided that they wouldn't hand in anything either. When the due date arrived, not a single student turned in the assignment.

Mrs. Finske was indignant. "A week! If you don't hand in your papers in a week, you will all fail this class!"

She marched out of the room.

"If I couldn't write it in a month, I definitely can't write it in a week," I said. "I guess I'll fail."

"You'll have to take the class again next semester," someone said.

"Yes, but if nobody else writes a paper I doubt Mrs. Finske will really fail the entire class. It wouldn't look good for her. Unity is strength," I added, a phrase I had learned in the Komsomol.

Mrs. Finske was obviously informed about this student meeting; in the afternoon, she asked to see me. I should clarify that I liked this woman. She was pretty and intelligent. I felt sorry for what was happening. We had coffee in the cafeteria.

"You can get the class to hand in those papers," she said.

"What makes you think that?" I asked.

"I'm not saying you caused the situation. But we're at a stalemate and you have the ability to get us out of it."

She said that if everyone handed in a paper at week's end—she didn't care if we copied verbatim from books, just so long as we handed in *written pages*—then we could further discuss the assignment in order for her to understand why everyone had found it difficult.

"We could've had that discussion in the first place," I suggested.

"I don't want to argue. I am asking you to do me a favor."

I had unwittingly become the leader of a strike and I wasn't even a student activist! I relayed Mrs. Finske's offer to my classmates.

"You mean we can just copy somebody else's work?"

"Yes. And it hardly seems to matter if the passages are appropriate to the assigment or not."

For my paper, I didn't plagiarize but wrote what little I thought I understood. I received an A+. *Good job!* Mrs. Finske had scrawled at the top of the first page.

In the West, individuals who prefer solitude are suspect, "loner" being a word often used to describe a neighbor who turns out a serial killer. But in other cultures, the loner is a heroic figure. The Samurai, for example. Although that might be more historical, because these days extroversion seems especially prized, everyone advertising themselves to the online world as much as their governments will allow, finding glory (or desperation) in the number of their social media followers.

Steve never needed many friends. He enjoyed being with people but rarely called anyone to suggest a get-together, preferring to keep to himself. I envied his contentment in his own company. When I say that I've always needed interaction with others to feel... if not happy, then okay, I am obviously referring to genuine, real-life interaction, not the kind that requires looking at a screen.

"If you need any help," friends say, "call me."

I have news: I need help but I won't call. In future, assuming I have one, should any of my friends find themselves widowed, I will call them regularly and ask if there is anything specific I can do for them *right then*. Or better, I will just do what I think needs doing. My help will not be conditional on whether or not they have the initiative to reach out; the burden will not be on the mourner.

Despite friends who mean well, despite my daughters, loneliness is my closest companion.

Social welfare organizations were new to the city. Agencies like the Red Cross, the Housing Authority, the YM/YWCA, and even the Family Services of Greater Hong Kong were only starting to get their footing. My Saturday classes gave way to fieldwork in the Family Services' central district office, where I started case files for those who came through the door—people living in the resettlements, mostly squabbling neighbors and couples at odds. I quickly came to understand that lack of decent housing and the struggle to merely subsist created a lot of conflict, and I began to doubt my decision to switch majors. It was one thing to want to help the poor and needy, another to know and accept what helping them required and how it impacted one's own life. By the time Alex returned from England in May, my doubt had increased. And although we didn't see each other as much as we would have liked—my semester wouldn't end until July and I had a heavy course load in addition to fieldwork—I found a minute to confess my misgivings to him.

"You only have one year left," he said. "Try to stick it out."

I didn't discuss my waffling with my parents, since I had changed my major without consulting them and I considered myself my own person, an adult.

When classes ended for the year, I continued working with Family Services, which was the only relevant placement for someone focusing on my kind of case work. Six days a week for ten weeks, I reported to the central district office. I'm not sure how it is now, but back then Hong Kong was a nocturnal city, with hardly anyone going to bed before midnight, a constant shooshing and honking of traffic, and music from night clubs that could be heard for blocks. I would get off work at five and meet Alex outside the theater at five-thirty, and after the movie—maybe a Civil War epic starring Gregory Peck—we would go to his parents' beach house to have sex. Or else we skipped the movie altogether. If Alex had family obligations, I would meet up with Au-Yeung and Bess, who didn't have to work and were spending a lot of time together without me.

"It's your own fault," Au-Yeung said.

Didn't I know it! But I had decided to take Alex's advice and "stick it out," mistakenly believing that I had experienced the worst of what fieldwork entailed.

"Did you hear?" a colleague asked me. "We're getting a new Director. She's transferring from the west district."

Details emerged over the next few days. Miss Tao, the new Director, was Shanghainese, an "old maid" in her forties. She spoke fluent English, had an undergraduate degree in social work from Columbia University in New York, and had spent two years in England learning the British social welfare system. According to gossip, she was the best educated, most experienced and demanding supervisor in all of Family Services, a hard grader and a slave driver, and she didn't approve of students sitting in the office, waiting for people to come through the doors; she wanted them out on home visits.

"You mean we'll have to go to the resettlements?" I asked apprehensively.

Not just that, said my ear-to-the-ground colleague. Miss Tao would expect us to go up into the hills to visit the squatters.

Auntie Amy's example notwithstanding, I accepted the cultural stereotype of the old maid, which shaped my first impression of Miss Tao even before I met her: she was a stern and heartless person, jealous of the young and attractive, and quick to criticize those who possessed what fortune and nature had denied her. And because the Shanghainese were known for having a certain air, a seemingly inborn sophistication, I let another crass generalization convince me that I knew the kind of woman she was: one who considered us Cantonese hopelessly rustic, backward. At times, life is governed by the crass and stereotypical.

On Miss Tao's first day, I arrived early to the office. I wore a navy blue *cheongsam* with a low split, and white flats. I carried a small white bag and wore my hair in a middle-length perm. My intention was to look refreshing and energetic, but *plain* so as not to offend the Shanghainese old maid Director. And instead of trying to be a charmer, which didn't come naturally to me, I planned to be as mute as possible. I had discovered, in work situations, that almost everyone liked you when you played dumb, or at least when you didn't constantly volunteer what you thought or knew.

At eight-thirty exactly, a tall slender woman with short straight hair, darkish complexion, and protruding teeth let herself into the office. She was smartly dressed and well made up, but these didn't enhance her features. She struck me as being tightly held, rigid with self-control. I had never encountered her like before—an old maid in a high position—and I was afraid of her.

Introducing herself to the office, Miss Tao said that she wouldn't hesitate to fail a student if she judged it appropriate, and yes, she wanted us solving problems out in the world, where life was lived, rather than waiting for needy people to come to us. I kept my eyes on her as if I were paying attention, but I found it difficult to concentrate. I was anxious because I didn't know if I could meet her expectations, and if I failed fieldwork, I wouldn't be allowed to graduate. But also, I was thinking, *My fieldwork director is an old maid. So is my case-work professor. Maybe my mother was right: I'll wind up an old maid, after all. Not because no man will marry a tomboy, but because that's what female social workers* are.

A woman called to report that her husband was being physically abusive, and Miss Tao sent me out to meet with her—my first real assignment. I took two buses to get to the foot of the squatters' hill and began trudging up a steep dirt path. Tin-roofed shacks arranged every which way slouched all around me. There were no street names or addresses. Dirty, scrawny, bent-backed people in tattered clothes eyed me as I passed. In my *cheongsam*, I must have looked like an apparition to them, maybe one from the better lives they had left behind when escaping the mainland. More than a few of these people..."accosted" is too strong a word. They insistently approached, asking for food, money, work. I wasn't frightened, but I was totally unprepared to feel so helpless in the face of such misfortune and acute suffering. What I knew of poverty, I realized with a shock, was terribly naïve. And the idea that had formed on the buses I'd taken to get there—that I would be like Alan Ladd in *Shane*, riding into town to do good deeds, then riding off again to do the same in another town—this idea began to crumble.

My client had described as best she could where she lived and said she'd be standing by a water drum at a certain corner. A water drum? Miss Tao had explained: daily, if not hourly, squatters had to carry water uphill and store it in old oil drums for their use. After an hour and a half of trekking past numerous water drums, I neared the top of the hill and thought I must have passed the meeting point. I was about to turn around when I saw her—in her late twenties probably, with a bruised right eye, and bruises on her left arm and neck, which she made no attempt to hide. Her two boys—aged one and three, I would soon learn—were with her, barely clothed.

Is it curious that I don't remember the woman's name? Telling, certainly. Though it was the heat of her personal story, her trials as an individual, and the painfully formal intimacy of our meeting that affected me that day, she has become an emblematic figure to me.

Her shack was indistinguishable from the others except for a splash of orange paint on the wall-boards alongside the entrance. Inside, there was no chair to sit on, only a single mattress on which her entire family slept.

"Would you like some tea?" she offered.

I took in the unsanitary conditions, the rust-scabbed tea kettle, the chipped porcelain cups that must have been salvaged from who knew where. I looked at her and found her unable to return my gaze.

"Yes, thank you," I said.

We remained standing with our tea while the boys played quietly on the mattress. I got her story out of her in fits and starts. She and her husband had escaped China just before their second son was born. Her husband worked odd jobs as a laborer, and she almost never left the shack. Lowering her voice and stepping toward the entrance as if to make it even fainter in the open air, she said that whenever her husband couldn't find work, he beat her, then demanded sex—all while the kids were awake.

She cried throughout our interview, and I had to continually remind myself that, as a professional, I needed to maintain emotional detachment to better assess and advise. But finally I couldn't help it; the tears came and I turned away to hide them.

"What can I do for you?" I asked.

"Please find my husband a job."

Now I was the one who couldn't make eye contact. I glanced at the jury-rigged, water-stained walls. In September, when the typhoons came, the family wouldn't even have their hovel to call home. What would her husband do then? But find him a job? Family Services wasn't an employment agency; we provided counseling. True, I might have referred the woman to the Red Cross for clothes, to Catholic charities for care packages, but could anyone help with a lack of employment? Besides, there were thousands of squatters who needed clothes and care packages and jobs, and more were coming daily. Every inch of open space between Hong Kong and Kowloon was taken up by refugees; Family Services didn't have the time or resources to help them all, and neither did the charities or the Red Cross.

The idea I had of myself as a maverick do-gooder like Shane fell away altogether; an overwhelming feeling of helplessness again came over me. The tea in my cup was cold.

"First," I said, adhering to protocol, "I need you and your husband to come to the office to further discuss your home situation."

She panicked. "I can't! He'd kill me if he knew I reported him!"

After some consideration, I said, "I have an idea how we can arrange it so he won't suspect you."

For the next hour, I walked about the area as if I were making rounds. When the husband returned—the woman, at her door, indicated him with the subtlest nod—I went up and introduced myself as a representative from Family Services.

"I'm here letting people know we can help them find jobs and better housing," I said. "If you just come to the office for an official interview and fill out some paperwork—"

But he refused. Steadfastly. Absolutely.

I lingered for some minutes afterward, unwilling to believe there was nothing I could do, and that night, feeling guilty and depressed, I couldn't sleep. I kept seeing the woman with her bruises, kept hearing her ask in a tone I have never been able to forget, "Please find my husband a job."

As strict as she was in professional matters, Miss Tao turned out not to have the shriveled heart of a spinster. She always treated us students to lunch and was equally generous with her knowledge, the lessons of her experience.

From our casual meal-time conversation, I found out that she had a younger sister who worked in the Hong Kong office of NCR, the National Cash Register Co., which was based in the States; also, that at Columbia University, she had been an admiring classmate of my mother's younger sister, Doris.

"A formidable mind," she said of my aunt.

Really? I didn't feel I was in a position to know, but I thought, *Oh great, now I definitely have to work hard to prove myself!*

Sometimes, the problems we encountered at Family Services came with us to lunch.

"But this is all temporary," I remember saying of the refugee issue, borrowing my mother's old phrase. "The government will have to establish more comprehensive programs and devote more resources to help these people."

Miss Tao smiled patiently, knowingly. "No matter the country, city or town, there are never enough resources or solutions for the problems a social worker faces," she said.

"Then why do it?"

"That's a question you have to answer for yourself. I do it because I must."

Miss Tao's rigor, her tightly held manner: I was coming to view these not as faults typical of a pinched old maid, but as the necessary demeanor of an impressive woman who understood the seriousness of the business she was embarked upon, and the importance of readying the next generation of social workers for the challenges ahead of them.

Throughout the summer, I made repeated trips to squatters' hills dressed in my *cheongsam*. My desire to alleviate people's suffering grew with every visit, but it was becoming increasingly apparent that the theories I learned in classrooms weren't all that useful. How could I help a couple deal with the psychological aspects of physical abuse, for example, when securing food and shelter was their primary concern? What to do when pathologies were caused by greater societal ills and the maladaptive coping methods of people bearing the brunt of those ills?

I went to see my first client again. I arrived at the tiny shack with its orange-spattered board, but she and her family were no longer living there. The new occupants didn't know where they had gone. Neither did any of the neighbors. That clinched a decision I'd been mulling: I had to do more, and to do more, I had to learn more.

What my classes at Chung Chi taught might have seemed unworkable in the real world of 1958 Hong Kong, but that didn't mean the same would be true for what was taught in classes elsewhere, did it? I was about to enter my senior year. Most of my fellow students intended to find local jobs after graduating. Only a handful—all boys except for Au-Yeung—were interested in going on to graduate study. That day, I became one of them. But nowhere in Hong Kong or Taiwan were MSW degrees awarded.

"I visited the US Consulate," I told my parents at dinner.

They looked at each other.

"Why?" my father asked.

"To research colleges in America."

My mother stopped eating and was slow to speak. "Wouldn't

you prefer to stay and find work in Hong Kong?"

She was, I suspected, thinking of Bentham and how she had lost him to communism.

"I'll come back," I said. "The whole point is to go and learn things to help the people here. So many of them are desperate."

Even as I said this, I knew my mother wouldn't believe it; she had heard it before. Her sister Lily had gone to the States for graduate study, with the intention to return and do some good in China; as had her brother Guy, who, after graduating from Nanjing University, attended dental school at USC. For Guy, it was the Japanese War that had kept him from returning; for Lily, it was love. Then there were also my father's brothers: Wu, puttering about in San Francisco, and Chung, who'd been prevented by World War II from returning to China after getting a medical degree from Johns Hopkins. And Uncle David, who had studied in France and was practicing law in New York. Of all my mother's siblings and in-laws who'd gone abroad, only she and Auntie Doris had come back to live.

"By the time you get a degree," my father said, "the people might not be so desperate."

Theoretically, this was true, but I deemed it unlikely. There were never enough resources, Miss Tao had said. The refugees of Hong Kong, among others, would still be in need.

My parents and I said no more on the subject that night, or for many nights afterward. I wrote to Uncle Albert, detailing the situation in the city and my desire to work with the poor and unfortunate to improve their lot. Could he help me find available fellowships in social work at universities in California? I asked. It so happened, he answered my letter in person while on a business trip to Hong Kong.

"I'm donating two scholarships a year to USC for Chinese students pursuing their graduate degrees," he told me. "If your grades are top-notch, I'll request that you get one of the scholarships. Mind you, you'll have to work extremely hard, and you'll need to get a part-time job to help support yourself."

"No one will work harder," I said.

Alex was happy for me. He was heading back to England at the end of summer to finish his master's, and our parents wanted us to get engaged, claiming that this would allow us both to focus on our graduate studies. They had it all reasoned out: after I earned my MSW, I would return to Hong Kong and marry Alex; we would go off and live for a time in England or the States, wherever he got his Ph.D., after which we'd come back to Hong Kong for good and Alex would inherit his father's business. Alex thought it was an excellent plan.

"I love you," he said.

I agreed to marry him, and we were engaged in August. We had a small celebratory dinner for family and a few close friends. Au-Yeung and Bess were there, and partway through the meal my mother leaned over to me and confessed her joy. She was relieved, she said, because my engagement to Alex meant that she and my father would never have to worry—I'd be leading a high-class life, not in America or anywhere else, but in Hong Kong, where my status would reflect most favorably on our family.

"Doesn't everything seem so right?" she sighed. "So perfect?"

8

NANCE OF THE SECOND CYCLE BEREAVEMENT GROUP advised me to keep busy.

"It will help distract you from the loss of Steve," she said.

But I don't want to be distracted, which seems disrespectful, too much like starting to forget. At the same time, though, I'm afraid that my grief is keeping Steve's spirit from being at peace. I remind myself of Big Bird's message—that he has settled in his next life— yet I can't help fearing that my behavior remains a burden to him.

Not just *my* behavior.

So much mail is still addressed to Steve, so many bills. I called GTE Mobile to get his name taken off the account. The representative said they would need his death certificate first.

"Why?" I said. "You're a phone company!"

A class should be taught in high school or college that prepares people for the various types of crazy that can swarm into their lives. Lesson number one: nothing might be wrong with you, but when everything going on around you is crazy, you won't be able to keep from reacting crazily.

The ultrasound and colonoscopy were clear: no cancer. My doctor prescribed Zoloft and admonished me to eat. I make an effort, but it's easier to stare at my food, feeling suicidal. I can't die until after two p.m. tomorrow, however, because acting on Nance's suggestion, and not wanting to weigh down Steve's spirit, I *am* trying to be busier. My days are like jigsaw puzzles, with me searching for pieces that fill in the blank hours. Tomorrow, I'll be volunteering at the Hong Fook Center, keeping the old and infirm company until midafternoon.

There's Matthew, the ex-soldier whose legs were blown off in combat and who has been left partially paralyzed by a stroke. On my previous visit, he told me that his diabetes medicine leaves him impotent. He cried in front of me over the loss of his manhood, his inability to express his love through a physical act and satisfy his wife.

More than one way to do that, I thought but didn't say.

There's Eileen, who is in her sixties and obsessively frets about the death of her eighty-year-old husband.

"Is he sick?" I asked.

"No, he's perfectly healthy for his age. But he's *eighty!*"

She said this with Ginny sitting only a few feet away—Ginny, who is eighty-six and resides in an assisted-living facility but apparently prefers the companionship she finds at the Hong Fook Center.

"The gravity of my life has changed," I said to her. "I feel heavy all over and it's hard for me to do anything." Still referring to myself, I said: "The patient exhibits an inability to incorporate loss."

Ginny nodded and her dry lips cracked into a smile, but she

didn't ask what I meant. I belatedly realized: mostly deaf, she had only seen my lips move.

I had expected to feel closer to Alex after our engagement, but I was uneasy. I alternated between wondering if I genuinely loved him and a state of awed disbelief because my situation seemed too good to be true. I would be Mrs. Alex Liu, with at least three maids in my household and a chauffeur-driven car at my disposal? I imagined myself sitting on the board of Miss Tao's Family Services, or being asked to officiate an opening ceremony for a new dorm at Chung Chi College. Alex's parents had been together for decades and seemed loving enough as a couple. Would I mellow into Mrs. Liu's soft-spoken, nurturing nature? Would Alex, like his father, want to delegate most domestic and social arrangements to me while he concentrated on business, in which he, too, would be smooth but not overtly dishonest?

I assumed that my doubts were normal for someone who had just made a momentous decision, and I kept them to myself. Alex left for England at the end of August, with the usual promises to keep in touch.

We called him Professor Plato—the minister from Toronto who taught philosophy my senior year. He was impatient with us because we never raised our hands. But asking questions in class didn't naturally occur to us. We had been brought up in what I consider a British style of learning, as opposed to American or even Canadian: we sat and listened, taking copious notes while a teacher lectured; then, on tests and in papers, we reported back what we'd been told. But there was, I think, an additional cultural aspect to our silence. In Chinese society, one speaks only when one has something knowledgeable to say, and we didn't know much about Plato or his *Republic*. We had no background in Western philosophy. So we kept quiet and wrote in our notebooks, and the deeper into the semester we got, the more upset Professor Plato became at our passivity.

"What's wrong with all of you?" he blurted in exasperation one day. "Can't anyone speak?"

Nobody answered.

He gave us an assignment to determine if we had absorbed any of the class material—we were to write the outline of a book report on *The Republic*. It was a difficult read for me, and I decided that instead of handing in an outline, I would make a diagram of what I thought I understood.

"That's not what the professor asked for," my classmates warned.

"He just wants to know if we understand the book," I countered.

Weeks went by, and finally, having looked over our assignments, Professor Plato said it was clear that some people had comprehended more of his lectures than others. He turned to the blackboard, but I stopped paying attention, needing to go over my casework for the upcoming Saturday. When I lifted my head at the end of class, I saw my diagram on the blackboard, and twenty-five years later, at an alumnae gathering in the States, I learned that Professor Plato had continued to use my drawing after I'd graduated, crediting it to a former brilliant student of his.

Brilliant? It isn't false modesty that induces me to say, *I don't think so*. I simply do what seems logical and efficient to me—and *for* me. The fact is, even now I'm uncomfortable recalling Professor Plato's praise. I have always found it difficult to believe I've done a good job on something, because whatever I do, it is never good enough.

I moved back home after the first semester. It was more convenient for my work at Family Services—now Wednesdays and Saturdays—and my frequent visits to the American Consulate, where I continued to research colleges. I planned to attend USC if I could, but I wanted to apply to other schools *just in case*.

Au-Yeung was also living at home, so we had more time together, without Bess, just the two of us on our commute to and from school.

"You should study in America too," I said.

From several boys in her department, she knew that there were a fair number of graduate fellowships available for chemistry students. I encouraged her to write to an uncle she had in the States and ask for his help. And guess what? Her uncle agreed to loan her the money to further her education overseas.

"I don't know if I can manage well there *and* repay the loan," she worried.

"Just get yourself to America and deal with the rest later," I said, because if she didn't finish school or pay back the loan (I knew she would succeed at both), what could her uncle do?

Our commute became a kind of study hall after that—Au-Yeung and I helping each other fill out graduate school applications and prepping for the English proficiency test we had to pass in order to get our visas. I'd been surprised by the strength of my desire to persuade, by how much it meant to me for her to come to America. It didn't matter if she wound up across the country from me. But why let an ocean separate me from my two best friends, if I could help it? *Yes*, I decided, *Bess should come as well. My magic carpet has room for all of us*. But these days, I think of it a little differently. It wasn't that my magic carpet had room so much as that I hoped Bess would realize she had a magic carpet too, that everyone did; they just had to get on and pilot it.

"Me, in America?"

Bess laughed and shook her head: it was impossible, unfathomable. Why? Because of family history and expectations, as is often the case with such self-limiting choices.

Bess's father had worked, along with his several brothers, in his parents' jewelry business. Leaving the store one evening—and this isn't a joke—he slipped on a banana peel in the street. He hit his head and died of brain trauma. He was twenty-nine years old. Bess's mother, a young widow with seven children to raise, had consequently lived in subservience among her in-laws. Bess was the second-oldest child; there was an elder sister and five younger brothers. Although she was a good student, Bess had been able to attend college only because her uncles had let her. But graduate school? No. They wanted her to find a job and get married, and Bess wasn't going to rebel when her older sister hadn't. So it seemed her life-path was to be an echo of Ngoi-Poi's: after her father died, my grandmother had obeyed her brother by traveling to Hawaii to marry Grandpa Ho; Bess, after her father's death, would similarly obey her father's brothers, but she would travel nowhere and marry...?

She was in a serious relationship with an unattractive young man from Shanghai. Au-Yeung and I thought she deserved somebody more handsome.

"Like Brando in *The Wild One*," I said.

"If you marry that guy, we won't come back from America to see you," Au-Yeung said, and I found myself nodding in confirmation: we absolutely would not come back.

In my fieldwork for Miss Tao, I continued to visit squatters' homes and resettlement areas, bewildered by the amount of suffering I saw, but not without optimism. Heroics were all around me: as frustrated, sad, angry, and destitute as people were, they refused to give up; they persisted.

I was, by then, thoroughly convinced that the theoretical material discussed in my classes was irrelevant to the population I served—a population contending with inadequate housing, unemployment, food scarcity, and a lack of schools. Western psychological theories, which were new to me and to the Chinese generally, and which were supposed to be part of my toolbox as a social worker, might have been scientifically true, but they offered nothing to people struggling to meet basic needs. I have said this already, I realize, but it's worth repeating.

I began to formulate my own methodology. Psychological theory could help me understand the overall framework of human behavior; I would let this inform but not dictate what I did on a practical level to achieve tangible improvements in the lives of those I served. Less consciously, my own coping mechanisms guided me as well: compartmentalization, containment, management of "symptoms." Oddly, my habit of repression, a habit typically considered a negative by therapists, paralleled a positive—the squatters' fortitude. Like them, I frequently detached myself from a less-than-ideal present by letting hopeful ideas about the future sustain me.

Too often, there wasn't much I could do except listen to the squatters' complaints and worries. But I genuinely desired to ease their cares and they sensed this. Little as they had, many of them wanted to show their appreciation by sharing with me half a bun or some other precious item from a Red Cross care package. I had always assumed that my years of malaria-induced isolation and my lonely, penned-in early and mid-teens had weakened my ability to connect with others—Chan Pei, Au-Yeung, and Bess were exceptions. But in fieldwork, my background was proving to be a benefit: I identified with the refugees because I knew what it was to be vulnerable and alone. Maybe this was why social work began to feel less like a pragmatic choice I'd made based on job opportunities, and more like a calling. Helping people, no matter how inadequately, fulfilled me in a way nothing ever had. I decided to devote my life to alleviate human suffering, of whatever kind, and however I could.

But what about Alex, whose agenda was to emulate his father, to become an engineer and have his own construction firm? Could I be married to a rich guy and still fight for those in need and find meaning in the fight? Of course. Except that, first and always, I would be Alex Liu's wife, Mr. Liu's daughter-in-law, which meant

I would more or less—but rather more—be doing social work as if it were a hobby. It would not be *the course of my life*.

There was no middle ground, as far as I could see: I had to choose between my fiancé and my life's purpose.

I wrote a letter to Alex, detailing what I could of my aspirations and my concern that our being together might keep me from fulfilling them. I openly questioned if our continued relationship would bring about happiness for both of us.

"We're perfect for each other," he wrote back, a line straight out of Hollywood, "and after we're married, you'll be in a better position to help people. You'll join organizations at a higher level and steer their policies."

He was right. My ability to effect change *would* be much more limited if I were just a social worker—without wealth and connections. But the big, amorphous dreams I spoke of earlier, I now knew, had little to do with my living a life of pleasure and ease and everything to do with being of service to others. And for that, I needed to be among those for whom I was working to effect positive change, rather than above them.

Tempted by money and status, I had forgotten my resolve not to become a mere adjunct to a man. To be plugged into a ready-made life, with my role pre-defined, felt dishonest, even fraudulent to me.

Of course, I still didn't understand what marriage was, or the sacrifices that it required. I had no idea what raising children or working for a living truly entailed. But I *would* make my own way in the world, I decided, and if I ever had a husband and partner, he'd have to be a soldier in the trenches with me, not a general bunkered a safe distance from the front line.

The Chinese are family-oriented. To counsel an individual and not involve his or her siblings, parents, aunts, or uncles seemed remiss to me when, after earning my MSW, I started working at the International Institute of Los Angeles. Especially as I had been hired primarily to liaise with other Chinese, who, like the squatters in Hong Kong, wanted more of a relationship with me than was professionally appropriate. A few times, in the beginning, I said to them that they shouldn't feel obligated to me for trying to help, that they didn't need to offer me favors or gifts, I was just doing my job. But I soon realized this was a mistake. If you tell a Chinese patient that therapy with you is strictly business, you will lose them. There has to be some personal *give* on the therapist's part, to earn their trust and help them feel less emotionally dependent. I couldn't treat them as if they were mere "cases."

In addition to Chinese, I wound up counseling a lot of refugees from Communist regimes—Hungarians, most notably.

In World War II, Hungary had initially been aligned with Nazi Germany, Fascist Italy, Romania, and Bulgaria, then tried to switch sides to the Western Allies. This of course had angered the Germans and they moved to take over the country, which the Soviets prevented from happening. The Hungarian People's Republic was subordinate to the Soviet Union after the war, but in 1956, the populace revolted—the so-called Hungarian Uprising. It was quashed by Soviet troops, although not before thousands had been killed and nearly a quarter-million had fled the country.

The Hungarian refugees I met in America were having trouble. Under communism, their entire lives had been controlled, everything provided for them—housing, food, clothes. But here, given a sum of money per month in assistance and left to do as they would, they were at a loss, not knowing how to budget for groceries and utility bills, how to efficiently exercise the most basic freedoms that, for many of us, are all too easy to take for granted.

"No other man is in my life," I told Alex when he came home for Christmas in 1958, "but I can't be connected to you, not to anyone." I reiterated what I had said in my letter.

"But don't you see that our marriage will make it easier for you to achieve your goals?" he asked.

I didn't. And to be honest, I *was* confused. On the surface, what I was doing made no sense. Unwilling to compromise, I was throwing our relationship away for a vagary, an inchoate pursuit.

Again and again, I explained that one of my goals was to carve a path on my own, but Alex refused to take it in. Why couldn't I help the poor and unfortunate as his wife? he kept asking. Our repetitions were getting us nowhere. I was tired. I loved him, just not more than I loved myself. I slipped off my engagement ring and held it out to him. Exasperated, he shook his head.

"Hold on to it until I come back in May. If you feel the same then as you do now, I'll take it."

He was an engineer; he believed in sound reasoning, logic, and must have thought once I'd had more time to consider, I would realize how impractical I was being.

"But please," he added, "let's not say anything to our parents until May."

"Okay," I agreed, knowing that I would not change my mind.

We informed our parents before Chinese New Year: we had broken off our engagement. They were predictably disappointed. Alex's parents worried that he wouldn't be able to concentrate on finishing his studies and might not want to meet other girls for a while. My father, resigned to the roadblocks that kept our family from getting ahead, sat in a haze of cigarette smoke and quietly said he wished it had worked out for us. My mother wasn't ready to accept that it hadn't.

"You don't love him?" she asked in private.

"No," I said. "Yes. I don't know."

She didn't argue on behalf of mutual love, instead saying that Alex's love was enough to make it work. How could I get her, of all people, to understand what I couldn't adequately justify? I did try, doubting myself all the while: it wasn't a matter of love, I told her, at least not in the way that she thought; it was a matter of the kind of life I needed to have in order to be most useful to others. Less dismissive than I had expected her to be, she echoed my own qualms, that I was throwing away an excellent situation for an uncertain future, and for once I couldn't argue with her.

"I'll set him up with Bess," I said to Au-Yeung.

"Who?"

"Alex."

"That's crazy."

Had she changed her mind about Bess's Shanghainese boyfriend?

"It would be weird to date, never mind marry, a best friend's ex-fiancé," she said. "And it's probably not smart to interfere in Alex's personal life right after you've called everything off."

No, probably not. Besides, although they'd have made a handsome couple, they were both so impressionable that Alex's mother would undoubtedly have been the leading partner in the relationship.

Hearing that Alex and I had broken up, Au-Yeung's fellow chemistry major Kao stepped up his pursuit of me, which he hadn't abandoned even after my engagement. Taught to distrust passionate, impulsive love, as so many of us had been, Kao's idea of romance took the form of persistence: fate would bring us together. In others, it took the form of sacrifice. We had all heard the countless stories of men killing themselves over thwarted love—stories that glorified the men. If one was disappointed in love, it was acceptable to choose death, which was looked upon as courageous rather than cowardly. I didn't think I was worth anybody killing himself for, but who was I to judge? When a melancholic started dedicating sad poems to me, I was careful not to give positive encouragement but remained friendly toward him, worried about what he might do to himself. I didn't concern myself too much with what he might do once I was across the ocean, assuming he would set his sights on someone else.

"My friends tell me that Hong Kong girls are in great demand in California," my mother said to me after the reality of my break-up had finally sunk in.

As if trying to convince herself, she talked of how the parents of American-born Chinese, or ABCs, preferred their sons to marry girls from Hong Kong, since they could converse with such girls in Cantonese.

"There's an excellent chance you'll make as good a match as Alex, or better," she said. "Young men wait at the airports just to meet girls from here. They introduce themselves and offer to drive you to your university or wherever you need to go."

"Are you encouraging me to get in cars with strange young men?" I asked.

I didn't pay a lot of attention to her stories, not caring whether I had a boyfriend, too taken up with the idea that someday I would fulfill an important mission.

Freedom. Does anyone correctly understand this word? We live in societies governed by laws. And besides, living peacefully among people in a community requires mutual respect and an awareness that our actions affect those around us; we're never really able to do whatever we please.

At nineteen years old, in my last semester at college and no longer engaged to Alex, I believed myself completely free to pursue my destiny. And I thought that as long as I cautiously, prudently welcomed people into my affections only to the extent that doing so didn't compromise my goals, I would be free for the rest of my life.

Absolute freedom: an ideal, a thing for Plato.

9

PLEASE, GOD, maybe it would be best if the man who loves me is unemployed, I used to pray.

Steve, my partner in the trenches, was a workaholic. While at USC, he had his studies, his Saturdays and odd afternoons at his father's store, and his duties in the Navy Reserve, which he had joined to avoid being drafted and sent to Europe during the Berlin Crisis—that blustery standoff between US-supported West Germany and the Soviet-backed East, which culminated in 1961 with the Soviets and East Germans erecting the Berlin Wall.

In his final months at college, Steve was urged by one of his professors, a superior in the Reserve, to apply to naval officer's school in Newport, Rhode Island. He was accepted but first wanted to get some work experience, so while still a student he found a part-time job at an architecture and engineering firm. The experience he hoped for didn't materialize; he was relegated to fetching coffee, cleaning toilets, and occasionally being allowed to draw a doorknob.

"People who look like me are only used as draftsmen," he

complained. "They never get to design anything or meet with clients."

Among his fellow classmates, those who looked like him weren't faring better at other firms. I had been at the International Institute for three years by that point and was pregnant with my elder daughter, not sure how much fieldwork I would be able to do in the upcoming months. After Steve's graduation, we decided it was time for him to begin his training at the Officer Candidate School, so he drew his last doorknob for his employer and off we went.

I don't remember thinking that I was sacrificing my career for his.

In 1959, the Communists still occasionally allowed people to pass in and out of the bamboo curtain, and my brother, whom I hadn't seen for more than half my life, was permitted to come to Hong Kong for two weeks. I never heard anyone ask why he was allowed to visit. Possibly my parents didn't care, thinking it would just be nice to have him home.

A tall, lanky, handsome man entered the flat—an adult I didn't recognize, a stranger. The lack of recognition was mutual. Bentham admitted it was hard to believe I was his little sister.

"I remember a feisty, strong-minded girl who was nasty to maids," he said.

Yes, but there I was, looking like a fairly reasonable adult in a cherry *cheongsam*, with a nice hairdo. My brother was used to seeing women in Mao suits—a sort of military uniform consisting of a tunic with two large breast pockets, two large hip pockets, and five buttons that were inevitably buttoned all the way up to a close-fitting collar. Worn by men and women alike, this plain suit was a sign of proletariat unity.

"You're beautiful," he said. "If you weren't my sister, I'd want to marry you."

His Cantonese was rusty; he'd been speaking Mandarin on the mainland. His demeanor was different too—less refined, more blunt. He acted like a proletariat, which to modern ears probably sounds snobbish. How can I give an adequate example of what I mean? I don't know if it's possible, but I remember that he ate fast, as if performing an unavoidable task and taking no pleasure in it, and he stared at people in a way that his former self would have considered rude or weird.

He followed me everywhere in the flat, even standing at the bathroom door to watch me comb my hair and put on my makeup. He kissed me on the cheek and touched me whenever he could, as if to make sure of a newly discovered treasure.

After a few days, I found out why he'd been allowed to come to Hong Kong.

Standing at the bathroom door, watching me comb my hair, he said, "I told my unit leader that my sister was graduating from college and I wanted to persuade her to return with me to serve China."

The Officer Candidate School program lasted sixteen weeks. Mindful of my developing pregnancy, I volunteered at the Red Cross, where my main job was calling field commanders to negotiate for soldiers' leave when their wives were about to give birth.

Steve and I were back in California, living in Port Hueneme, by the time our first daughter was born—at St. John's in Ventura, since the naval hospital was full, with so many sailors and officers starting or adding to their families, taking advantage of the fact that it charged just $7 for everything. When my daughter was a few months old, we left Port Hueneme for Camp Pendleton—a desert, a place of boredom. The first time I smelled a skunk, I mistook it for wildflowers and thought *I am not going to like this*. I didn't. Grocery shopping was the big entertainment. We lived there for two years before Steve requested a transfer to Treasure Island in San Francisco Bay. I became pregnant again and we bought our first house—in the Montclair area of Oakland Hills—paying $159 a month. Not as financially independent as I wanted to be, we'd had to borrow $7,000 from Steve's parents for the down payment.

"Stay in Hong Kong. Don't go back," my parents begged Bentham. "You can work in a hospital for a few years under British-educated MDs, then become a practicing MD here yourself."

He refused, determined as ever to give himself to China. He still had confidence that real change was underway, not just a transition from one corrupt government to another. But he had a more personal reason for refusing to stay: a serious girlfriend, a Communist Party member who worked as a nurse at his hospital. He'd been allowed to leave the mainland only because his girlfriend—soon to be his fiancée—had personally guaranteed his return. None of us was sure what such a guarantee meant, but it sounded ominous. Who was she, this woman willing to sacrifice herself in a test of his loyalty?

"She comes from a peasant family in Shandong," was all Bentham said.

He dreamed of becoming a full-fledged Communist Party member, like her, so that he could better serve China. *Better in what way?* I wondered. As a surgeon, what could he do as a Party member that he wasn't already doing?

"I applied for membership last year but was turned down," he told me.

"Why?"

He shrugged. "I have a bourgeois background, a sister and parents in Hong Kong, and too many relatives in the US."

I was furious when I heard this. He had gone to the mainland for his education and dedicated himself to his country, sacrificing his relationship with his family, and the Maoists told him, *No, you are too bourgeois to be one of us. You are not pure. We don't want you in the Party, but we do want you to stay in China and work for the people.* Meanwhile, in Macau and elsewhere, the Komsomol were no doubt recruiting bourgeois youths to be "undercover." It was ironic: my brother voluntarily endured the hardships of revolution and was devoted to the Communists' cause, yet they wouldn't let him—at twenty-nine years old—become one of them; whereas I had stayed in Macau and Hong Kong, never really turning my back on my bourgeois background, and been offered full membership in the Communist Party at sixteen!

I said nothing, thinking it would hurt Bentham to know I'd been accepted where he hadn't. But wouldn't *that* have been a good thing for him to learn? Wouldn't it have served as an example of Mao's hypocrisy, and so a reason for him not to blindly support the Communists and reconsider staying in Hong Kong? Possibly. But more likely, he would have considered me a fool for having refused such an honor.

"Alabama?" I said when Steve told me he was being sent there for a month.

Unpacked boxes were in every room of our new house in Oakland Hills. Our furniture looked unsettled, as if not sure of its proper place. I put my hands on my belly, feeling the baby.

Steve was an ensign in the Navy's construction battalion. What did Alabama have to do with the Navy?

"It will go by quickly," he said.

I had a miscarriage the night he left, after I bent down and struggled to open the manual garage door. The fetus, a male, had been four-and-a-half months old.

The weeks did not pass quickly. They were weeks of self-recrimination and sadness, weeks of feeling hollowed out, and as kind and loving as Steve was on the phone, they were a lonely trial. I was convinced that although I had done nothing wrong, I was at fault for losing our baby. I tried not to let my depression affect how I mothered my daughter, a living reminder of what I'd lost.

I came out from putting my elder daughter to bed one evening and found Steve, newly back from Alabama, working at the dinner table, sketching, murmuring.

"Critical path activity. Crashing Critical Path. Optimistic Time. Pessimistic Time."

At first I assumed he was working on an official project, but there was something in his intensity...

"What're you—?"

He looked up. "What's our main financial goal?" He didn't wait for me to answer and flourished a sheet of paper, on which he'd sketched a strange diagram. "To be millionaires by the time we're forty. And this is how we get there."

He'd drawn a Project Evaluation and Review Technique—or PERT—chart, a project-management tool he had learned about while he was away.

Looking at his diagram, I saw a bunch of circles and boxes with words like "income" and "investments" and "expenses" in them. Nodes, he said they were called. Arrows branched out from these nodes to others that contained dollar amounts—"$100,000," "$200,000," etc., up to a million.

How this doodle, which represented an interlinked series of tasks, was supposed to propel us to millionaire status, I had no idea. But from that night on, we subjected every expenditure to the PERT chart, which both directed and mapped our budgeting, our pains-taking step-by-step accumulation. Over two decades, we never had anything but modest salaries, and on the rare occasions we ate out, it was at the same Chinese restaurant, where, for the first number of years, a bowl of wonton noodle soup cost seventy-five cents.

Critical Path Activity: a task that can't be delayed without impinging on other tasks. *Crashing Critical Path*: when the completion time of a task is shortened.

These once cryptic phrases became as familiar to me as my own name.

Optimistic Time: the minimum amount of time required to complete a task. *Pessimistic Time*: the maximum amount of time required to complete a task.

What does it mean when I say that I never really counted my

blessings while Steve was alive, yet if I remember correctly, I often wasn't happy?

"You can teach English, if nothing else," Bentham said.

"Why would the Party want me to teach the language of colonialism?" I asked.

He had no answer. He was just saying whatever he thought would convince me to return to China with him, unable to appeal to social work because the Communists didn't believe in it; such things were required only in a capitalist society, where greed had no mercy and created ills that welfare programs attempted to rectify.

"The Communists are striving for a utopia," I told Bentham. "It won't work and history will prove me right."

"You're a reactionary," he said to me angrily, "an anti-revolutionist! You've been brainwashed by the colonizers!"

There had always been a conflict in my family between East and West. We were trying to live a traditional, bourgeois Chinese lifestyle but were informed by Western habits and ways of thinking handed down from the British and Portuguese. White society had said to us: So what if Grandpa Ho had grown up in Hawaii and some of his children were born there? So what if your father and uncles and aunts were educated at Ivy League universities? You are not one of us. No wonder Bentham strove to be "authentically" Chinese. But we weren't that either and never could be; our very thinking had been colonized.

A reactionary. An anti-revolutionist. Brainwashed.

Bentham's words were similar to those hurled at me by Chan Pei years before, but—no matter that I hardly knew him, he was my brother and I wanted his approval—they hurt more coming from him. He made me feel like a traitor. I nearly blurted that I'd been in the Komsomol and had had what he so desperately wanted, an invitation to be a Party member—me, his little sister, whom he followed around the flat and watched comb her hair.

While Steve spent his days on Treasure Island studying the effects of biowarfare, monitoring the recovery of Vietnam soldiers exposed to Agent Orange, I had somehow become a stay-at-home mom. In the afternoons, I frequently met with other young mothers, several of whose children, like my elder daughter, were American citizens by virtue of their birth. Some of these women were Chinese, but not all.

From my work at the International Institute of Los Angeles, which offered legal services to immigrants, I knew that a quota system was in effect and only 105 immigrants from the Asia-Pacific circle were admitted within a given year, while the limits for Germans and other Western Europeans was in the 10,000s. Also, I knew that there was a hierarchy of preference for the sort of Asians who were admitted, with parents at the top, brothers and sisters next, followed by those who filled specific gaps in the workforce.

One of my friends wanted to know if a relative with a mental illness could become a citizen. Not a question with a simple answer, because of course it depended on the illness—depression or schizophrenia, for example—and myriad other factors of a given person's situation. I told her that I didn't know, but I would research it for her, and I'd also find out how the immigration quota might affect my other friends, who, to better protect their children, were eager to become US citizens, which Steve and I already were.

I phoned the International Institute of East Bay, explaining who I was and my reasons for calling. Learning that I had an MSW and was bilingual, the intake worker put me on hold.

"I hear you're looking for a job," the Director said, coming on the line.

Her name was Zoe, and she was eager to hire a Chinese-speaking MSW.

"Someone to go to Chinatown and find out what problems there are and what resources they have," she said. "Would you be interested?"

The Treasure Island naval station had childcare. I started working two days a week.

Bentham stayed with us in Hong Kong for almost three weeks. My parents and I went to the train station to see him off. What would he say to his unit leader about me? About his failed recruitment mission? Would he be punished?

You can tell yourself that you won't give up your dreams for someone else's, but as Bentham's train pulled out of the station, my anger and disappointment with him faded. We had nothing in common except family ties. Where he was quiet and submissive, I was expressive and bold—"feisty," as he'd put it. Where he believed in the purity of the Maoists' motives, I did not. But although I was critical of his belief, it was also what I liked best about him: his devotion, his dedication to being a "people's doctor." So I guess I misspoke. We *did* have something else in common: the need to work on behalf of those less fortunate. And as his train gathered speed and his thin face shrank into the distance, I suffered a momentary pang. *I've made a mistake!* I thought. *I should have gone with him! Then surely they would admit him into the Party!*

Bentham and I had no direct communication over the next sixteen years, and for much of that time my parents once more had to get what little news of him they could from Po-Po, my step-grandmother in Canton. This because China slid into chaos, starting with the Great Leap Forward, which turned out to be more like two steps back, and which bled into the Cultural Revolution with its purging of "bourgeois infiltrators" and all things capitalist, the Red Guards rooting out those they deemed not "sufficiently revolutionary"—in other words, anyone they suspected of even respectfully disagreeing with Mao's policies.

Newly hired by the International Institute of East Bay, I went to Oakland's Chinatown and introduced myself to community organizations, religious leaders, family associations, and the tongs. I didn't care whether or not a tong was involved in organized crime, since whatever else they did, they were helpful to local residents, providing immigration advice and English tutoring, and in some cases running Chinese schools. As I made my rounds, I couldn't help noting the differences between me and many of the people I met. Some, though they had been born in China, had grown up in the Bay Area and hardly spoke Cantonese or Mandarin. Recent immigrants seemed dazed by the American consumer-scape and way of doing things, not having come from a West-inflected family, as I had. But what I saw in them, perhaps others—those born and educated in America, fluent in English as well as the Chinese of their parents—saw in me. After all, I wasn't far removed from the days when, fresh off my magic carpet, I found myself living with nine other women in a co-op established by Uncle Albert on USC's fraternity row, democratically sharing the responsibilities of cooking and cleaning and grocery shopping, the latter especially difficult for me because I was unfamiliar with the merchandise and didn't fully comprehend US currency.

My observations of cultural differences within Chinatown informed my assessment of the community's needs, but they were, to my mind, more of a personal nature; I was interpreting what I saw in relation to myself. In a blatantly professional sense, my fieldwork revealed that, while people came to the International Institute for legal aid, many of them had family, medical, or mental health problems. Unsurprising, really. An immigration process that separated families for eight to ten years created challenging—not to say traumatic—situations: children grew up without parents, either one or both, in the second case living with a distant relative; and spouses grew apart when one emigrated years before the other, assimilating to the point that they were virtually a stranger to the newly arrived partner. Outside the community, however, the general belief was that Chinese people didn't suffer mental health problems—a belief compounded by the fact that, for community members themselves, mental illness per se didn't exist. A depressed person was just considered quiet; a bi-polar person, moody or short-tempered; an autistic person, eccentric. The Chinese didn't recognize symptoms of psychoses and had no vocabulary for discussing such issues, even if they wanted to. I saw a need for the International Institute of East Bay to branch out into social services.

"The problem is funding," my boss Zoe said, sympathetic but encouraging. "Why don't you write a proposal for a pilot project to establish the program you think is necessary?"

I had trained to be a case-worker, a counselor who visited and talked with patients. What did I know about writing proposals?

Bess was apprehensive about her future. Her two best friends would be going to America and the best job she could line up after graduation was in a money exchange company, where she would sit in a cage like a casino cashier. These exchanges had outposts all over Hong Kong to accommodate tourists, typically in jewelry stores. Bess had been offered a salary of $250 a month—at the high end of the range—because she was an honors student.

"There aren't other jobs available," she said when I reminded her that, as a trained bookkeeper, she was overqualified. "Banks want to hire people with experience or a degree from England."

"You're underselling herself. You should look for work in foreign companies with offices in Hong Kong."

Pretty and easy-going as she was, I thought her the kind of young woman that foreign bosses would like for an administrative assistant or secretary.

"My English isn't good enough," she said.

An intelligent, attractive woman lacking self-confidence: not a new phenomenon.

Through a friend of my mother's, I secured Bess an interview at AIA, the American International Assurance Company.

"I can't work in insurance!" Bess protested.

I might have known. Among the more conventional or rural

Chinese, superstitions persisted. For my friend and her family, any talk about dying—theirs or somebody else's—was bad luck. To work in the life-insurance industry would have been inviting death into their inner circle.

My mother apparently had no such fears or else felt that she couldn't afford them. My father was often home in those days, uncommunicative, playing solitaire for hours, which meant he was having money problems. How we knew this when he refused to talk about our finances—nobody was allowed to ask; he was the breadwinner and didn't want to share his burden—I can't say. In any case, my mother had started to work at AIA as a salesperson, a position that required patience and a willingness to educate a skittish public. What she had was a lot of friends, many of whom were less superstitious than Bess's family and wound up buying policies through her.

Here in America, we buy only what we want and don't bother with what we'd rather not have; our friendships have little or nothing to do with it. But in China, if a person is nice to you, offering you something with the best intentions, you accept it to return the favor of their regard—even if you don't need or approve of it. For example, say you don't want life insurance but your friend comes to you as a salesperson. Say, also, that the typical policy pays out twenty thousand dollars. Because you want to be supportive of your friend, you might buy a policy worth five thousand dollars, or you'd buy the typical coverage and decrease it over time.

My mother, fearing poverty more than death, taking advantage of a polite culture, sold insurance to Ginling alumnae while my father sat home with his deck of cards, saying nothing of her employment.

With AIA not an option for Bess, I turned my thoughts elsewhere and remembered that Miss Tao's younger sister worked at the National Cash Register Company. NCR was an American concern with its own office complex near downtown and a product selling extremely well on account of Hong Kong's tourist business.

"Is it all right if I reach out to your sister on Bess's behalf?" I asked Miss Tao after detailing my friend's situation.

"Can't she apply for jobs on her own?"

In this, I heard other questions: Why should I concern myself so much with Bess's future welfare? Wasn't it presumptuous of me to think I knew better than she herself did? How would I have felt if my friend were lobbying companies for me without my knowledge?

Well, I *was* being presumptuous, and I wouldn't have liked it if my and Bess's roles had been reversed, but I couldn't help treating her like one of my Family Services cases, even though she was better off than all of them. It's what social work had taught me— that I got great satisfaction tending to other people's needs, trying to protect them, to ensure they were healthy and secure. In the caretaker's role, I was able to become the person I felt I'd never quite had in my own life.

I phoned the younger Miss Tao, who was NCR's Manager of Demonstration & Distribution in the East. Her boss, an American man of middle age, frequently traveled to other parts of Asia for work and left her with a free hand to hire entry-level staff.

"I could use a business major in my department," she said, hearing about Bess. "Her degree will help give clients confidence in our products."

She explained that Bess would have to go through a training program, during which her salary would be $225 per month, but after that it would increase to $250. Bess would be eligible for further raises after six months. If she excelled, she could make good money, but there was also a chance she could be dismissed from the training program.

"Bess is smart and dependable," I said, confident that she would excel *if* I could get her to take the job.

Her initial reaction was not enthusiastic. "I'd be paid less," she complained, "and demonstrating cash registers isn't making the most of my degree either."

"The lower salary's temporary," I reminded her.

"It's a large company," Au-Yeung put in, wanting to convince her almost as much as I did.

"Work in your usual responsible way and there will be more opportunities for raises and jobs than with *the cage*," I said, which was what I called the money exchange place.

Still, Bess hesitated.

"Take the risk," I urged. "If it doesn't work out—and that will only happen if you don't want it to—the other kind of job will be waiting for you."

She and I had lunch with the younger Miss Tao. The NCR offices were spacious and gleaming and evoked serious business in a way that a downtown jewelry counter never could. The younger Miss Tao was slender like her sister, with the same short, straight hair, but her teeth were better and she was freer in her movements, not as militant about being the exemplar of a professional woman. She talked animatedly about her department, about NCR and its employee benefits. Bess accepted the job, and Au-Yeung and I took her out to celebrate.

It was spring, the weather starting to get humid, time flitting along, and our hearts were throbbing with what was to come: Au-Yeung and I off on a faraway continent, Bess setting foot in a new world although remaining in Hong Kong. Yet in the midst of our celebration—a meal, a bit of fun at the campus villa reminiscent of old times—doubt overcame me: Had I irrevocably broken up with Alex? Was I really leaving my parents and Ah Ying and going overseas? Ah Ying had been part of my life for almost as long as I could remember, a more constant and supportive presence than either my mother or father, and it was hard for me to fathom being without her. Not just because she took care of me in a menial sense—ironing clothes, cooking meals, pouring tea. I had confided to her as to no one else; of friends and relatives, she was the only person who knew I'd been in the Komsomol. I had allied with her; for many years, we'd been the proletariats of the family, standing by each other every time my mother, the bourgeois mistress, was being unreasonable. In her necessarily servile way, Ah Ying had protected me as best she could when I'd been particularly young and defenseless. And in teaching her how to write, I had perhaps sparked my desire to be useful to society, so actually we had been each other's tutor as well as ally and friend. How could I survive without her? And wouldn't I miss Hong Kong's crowded streets, its unique shops and food vendors, its beautiful beaches? The city had shown me the true meaning of resilience. Could I say goodbye to a remarkably adaptive and hard-working people, and hello to America where...*what?*

I'm aware that I have sometimes made it sound as if I knew what I wanted from an early age—to fly off on a magic carpet to a land where new freedoms and opportunities awaited me. I *did* want to go to America, and I felt I had a mission in life and that it involved helping people, but I didn't know specifically how or when this mission would reveal itself to me. Wanting to do something, and having the courage to do it, aren't the same, and in memory, one's life-path appears straighter than it actually was. My floundering with Alex and my vacillations about my future were more profound and all-encompassing at the time. I frequently accused myself of being a hypocrite—a big promoter of others taking a chance on new frontiers, confident in their success, but less gung-ho and sure when such expanses were in front of me. This wavering, I know, was normal for the same reason why the prospect of leaving was exciting: if my fear of failure wasn't greater than my desire to *experience*, I would be venturing into the unknown.

10

ALEX CALLED TO TELL ME that he would be in Hong Kong to attend my graduation. I didn't want him there; if I had to say goodbye to him in person when I left for America, I wouldn't be strong enough to get on the plane.

"I thought you were going to take classes over the summer?" I said.

"I changed my mind."

"Or travel to Europe before coming back?"

"You don't want to see me." His voice wilted with hurt. "You have so much compassion for the suffering masses but none for the man who loves you."

Afraid of my own vulnerability, I had come off as heartless, telling him not to come home until I was gone.

To write my proposal for the International Institute of East Bay, as Zoe had encouraged me to do, I first studied older ones given to me by a volunteer fundraiser, and I gleaned that a successful proposal identified a problem, detailed a program to address that problem as well as methods of outreach, and articulated the program's goals and the means for evaluating its efficiency.

It was necessary, I wrote, to debunk the stereotype that Chinese didn't have mental health issues, since they put an avoidable burden on the city's resources. Not only in terms of emergency services and their cost, but also in lost productivity and revenue from people who weren't contributing as much to society as they otherwise could. "Economic problems beget emotional ones," I wrote—my old chestnut—and my proposed Chinese Community Council would advise people about employment opportunities and finances, as well as educate them about mental health and available treatments, referring those in need to the appropriate county resources. We would, in essence, provide data to corroborate the fact that the Chinese population indeed suffered from mental illnesses, just like "whites," which would help city and state officials craft effective social policy.

"Excellent," Zoe said, reading it over.

She sent the proposal to the San Francisco Foundation, who saw enough merit in it to donate seven thousand dollars.

In the spring of 1959, I started a photo album, filling it with pictures I'd taken of Hong Kong: its industries and resettlements, squatters' huts and people, including quite a few of my clients and their families. Interspersed among these, I laid in newspaper clippings about the city. I wanted my graduate school faculty and classmates in the US to know where I came from. I wanted to educate Americans about Hong Kong, its humanitarian problems and persevering populace.

"When you come back after your studies," Miss Tao said to me, "I can give you a high position, such as Director of a district office."

One of my social work professors said he'd like me to teach at Chung Chi upon my return. The American Women's Association, which had given me a scholarship my senior year—awarded to a female student in a Christian College who had excelled academically—expressed warm, optimistic predictions for what I would accomplish in the city. And the Red Cross was constantly on the lookout for a Cantonese-speaking MSW to take charge of a local chapter. So an abundance of impressive options—the promise of a great career—awaited me in my hometown. And I *had* told Uncle Albert that my motivation for going overseas was to get the expertise I needed to better help the refugees in Hong Kong. Plus, I could fall back on old friends, should I desire. Even though Au-Yeung would probably stay in the States—she intended to work in the pharmaceutical industry—Big Sis and Big Brother were nurses in the city. Tsang Shuet King, who had declared her love for me in middle school, was a teacher there. And then of course Bess would be at NCR. It wasn't that I had ruled out the possibility of returning to Hong Kong, just that I had to keep the immediate future top of mind, and my plan was to get my master's degree and a year or two of work experience in the US. Beyond that, I could be certain of nothing.

Alex wrote to say he wouldn't be at my graduation in May, after all. He wouldn't be coming back to Hong Kong before I left, having decided instead to attend a summer session at Oxford and then visit the Canary Islands and Italy. I assumed he packed his schedule out of consideration for me, not because he was hurt and angry that I had told him to stay away. But my assumption was obviously wrong. It *had* to be wrong; I hadn't adequately explained why I didn't want to see him—that it wasn't for lack of love but the opposite.

The Chinese Community Council operated under the auspices of the International Institute of East Bay, but I felt it important for us to be located in the heart of Oakland's Chinatown, and Zoe agreed, so I borrowed space in the community center and set up shop. I recruited a couple of volunteers, and a Chinese-American woman from the Employment Development Department came once a week to help people with applications for jobs and financial relief. Despite being the Council's founder, I too was essentially a volunteer, a consultant, earning only what I made as a part-time employee of the International Institute.

Initially, the Council was met with taciturnity and suspicion, very much as I had been by the refugees in Hong Kong. But whereas desperation had driven those refugees to openly ask for help, in Oakland no one wanted to admit to financial difficulties; it was considered shameful to have them and to ask for assistance. They were used to talking to village elders, if anyone at all, about their problems. I was in my twenties, an obvious member of the bourgeoisie, and I represented some council they had never heard of: What advice could I possibly provide? To earn people's trust, I had to give more of myself than was prescribed by classroom textbooks, walking a fine line between academic distance and emotional availability. I occasionally even confessed that I'd had a hard time after I left home, and that I had written to my father, telling him I doubted I could survive.

"And he replied with an old saying," I would recount, "that 'if Heaven wants you to do something bigger, first it will—'"

"'—tire your mind and body in preparation for the larger task,'" many of them finished.

Once a Chinese person accepts you as a counselor, therapist, or any sort of helping hand, they are unfailingly grateful. In later years, when I was doing case work rather than acting as a referral service, I was often treated like a member of a patient's family. But as I say, at this juncture I wasn't counseling patients, too busy getting the Community Council going and trying to secure additional funding for its continued existence. With Zoe's help, one of my financial appeals made it to the United Way, whose donation enabled the Council to move from its temporary space in the community center to the ground floor of an old sewing factory—a former sweat shop.

Momentum was picking up for my organization, but I wouldn't be there to shepherd it onward because I went on maternity leave. In 1968, I gave birth twice—first to the Council and then to my younger daughter, but when I returned to work after my months' long absence, I found that Zoe had, out of necessity, hired a replacement for me at the Council, and my relationship with it had forever changed.

In Chinese culture, as long as you're a good student, you have no problems, no right to be unhappy. But do poorly and fail to get into the best schools and you bring disgrace upon your family and might as well die. In 1950s Hong Kong, young people committed suicide all the time because of academic failure. But unlike cases of unrequited love, their deaths had no heroic connotations.

In my last semester at Chung Chi, my grades were uniformly excellent, which fostered the image that I was a sensible, responsible person when I felt as if I were full of loose, disconnected wires—a knotty mess. How I had become a top student, I didn't quite know. And everyone expected me to maintain my high standards; it was unspoken but omnipresent. It's like that with most things, isn't it? Once you are nice to people, they expect you to be nice. Once you are generous to people, they expect you to be generous. Once you are a good student, people expect you to always be a good student. I have never made my peace with it—how little any of us can be ourselves on a given day; how much we are molded, hemmed in, by the expectations of others.

Every marriage has its culture too. In the mid-1970s, on my birthday, Steve gave me a card: *Now that you're thirty-five, you can do whatever you want to do.* After twelve years together, we opened our marriage, allowing ourselves to date other people. Our only rule: we could spend a single night elsewhere with a lover, but not longer.

I don't think our daughters were aware of the arrangement. They have said they remember us arguing a lot, but we didn't tend to fight about lovers. I am afraid neither daughter will understand or believe that throughout it all, Steve and I remained faithful to each other, to the culture we had established for ourselves.

Everything in America was set. I had been accepted into UC Berkeley's School of Social Welfare and the George Warren Brown School of Social Work at the University of St. Louis, but I would be attending USC, my first choice. Uncle Albert promised to have his son-in-law pick me up me every Friday and bring me to Beverly Hills to spend weekends with him and Auntie Lily. Uncle Guy would be nearby, in a place called Baldwin Hills. Really, though, I hardly knew Uncle Albert. And I knew Uncle Guy even less, despite having heard stories about him for years—that he would have taken over Ngoi-Gung's dental practice in Nanjing if war hadn't prevented it; that as a professor of dentistry, he had the habit of whittling his chalk into a molar, which he would throw at any student who wasn't listening; that in private practice, he counted the actress Elizabeth Taylor among his patients, and she had once shown him a nine-carat diamond ring given to her by Richard Burton and teased, "Dr. Ho, if you can fit this ring on any of your fingers, it's yours!" But he couldn't, or at any rate he had pretended the ring didn't fit, not even on his pinkie. So yes, I was familiar with family folklore, and yet every day that I got closer to leaving Hong Kong, I prayed that my American dream wouldn't turn out a nightmare, with me friendless, a stranger among aunts and uncles. I couldn't sleep and lost weight.

"Maybe I won't go," I said to Au-Yeung one day, as casually as I could.

"Then I probably won't either."

"But what about your career?"

She shrugged. "You'll be the only person I know in America, and if I run into a serious problem, you'll have my back, but if you don't go…"

I never discussed it with her again.

Two years after the Chinese Community Council was born, I was again working directly with Zoe at the International Institute, still a part-timer, my hours spent at the office.

Zoe, who constantly found new means of support for those in need throughout the East Bay, was an innovator in the social services field, the ultimate advocate for anyone struggling to get a foothold on the lowest rungs of domestic security and comfort. She did more than restart my career by hiring me; she changed the course of it. Or maybe I should say that she widened its ground, giving me the tools and experience beyond what was strictly required of a case worker. But as much as I liked learning from her example in the office, I wanted to get out into the community, to start counseling one on one, as I had been trained to do.

"You're too valuable here," she said sympathetically.

She meant at fundraising, writing proposals.

"But the residents of Chinatown deserve more," I said. "The Community Council's a good start, but that's all it is—a start."

"What do you have in mind?"

The Council was strictly for *new* Chinese immigrants, and focused on gathering information and making the appropriate referrals as it was, it basically provided orientation services, very little of which, it had turned out, involved mental health. Why? New immigrants, struggling to meet the urgent needs of food and employment…well, *if* they had mental health issues, these weren't yet surfacing because of the pressure to just survive.

But the more I considered what I'd seen in the field among immigrants who had been here awhile—how, with their basic needs met, psychological problems reared up—the more appropriate an emphasis on mental health seemed. So I wrote a proposal for the Chinese Family Outreach Program, which would be available to *every* Chinese immigrant, regardless of how long they had been in the US. The Family Outreach Program would still focus on gathering information and making referrals, but with its more inclusive mandate, it would be better able to prove that the local Chinese were contending with mental health issues, and it would act as a bridge to getting them help, for the benefit of the East Bay.

After discussing things with Zoe, I sent my proposal to California's Department of Mental Hygiene, and when funding came through, I went to the former sewing factory and spoke to Pauline, the Chinese Community Council's Office Manager, who agreed to let the Family Outreach Program use the vacant second floor, rent-free. Steve, with his architectural know-how, turned that dusty nothing-space into a functioning office while I scavenged furniture from the county jail and a defunct youth center that had been run by a gang leader named Tom-Tom.

All of us at the Outreach Program worked part-time. Most were volunteers. We introduced ourselves to school officials and started meeting with troubled kids and their parents. We went around to state hospitals to get leads on Chinese patients. Historically, these hospitals had often kept patients for a long time—decades, and sometimes even for life. For that degree of care, there were significant out-of-pocket costs, which could put a strain on the finances and relationships of any family, but especially on immigrant families that made ends meet by operating small grocery stores or what have you. Some couples had to divorce so that the committed spouse could continue being treated at the hospital without putting a financial burden on the other. By the late 1960s, however, with the advent of psychotropic drug regimens, hospitals were able to release patients into their communities, to be treated by clinics and relevant agencies. Alameda County had a mobile mental health emergency services van, and through someone who worked on it, I met the Wolfman.

Wild-haired and bearded, Wolfman was living in a closet, urinating and defecating into a coffee can. His mother left his meals outside the door for him. It's not possible to cure everyone, of course. In many cases, there is no cure. As a social worker, you try to ease a client's situation and help them utilize available resources—by which I mean, whatever treatment options are available to them at outpatient clinics, Board & Care facilities, or group homes; their eligibility for financial assistance, such as Supplemental Security Income (SSI) or food stamps; and medication management. If possible, you meet with the client's family to coach them on how to supportively cope with their loved one. And if you're lucky, you get a Wolfman to emerge from his closet and do his business in a bathroom instead of a coffee can, then watch him peaceably go with the mobile crisis services unit you called, who take him to a psychiatric hospital, where he stays until he can be stabilized through drugs and talk therapy.

The Outreach Program's work attracted the attention of the Director of Alameda County's Children and Family Services Department, who also happened to work as a part-time consultant for the International Institute. Her name was Reiko, a Japanese War bride with an MSW. Impressed with what we were doing, she published an article about us in *Social Casework: The Journal of Contemporary Social Work*. Reiko and I started talking a lot about how to enhance the program, and before long, a logical extension occurred to us: Why not have a linguistically accessible and culturally competent mental health services resource, not just for the Chinese, but for the East Bay's entire Asian population?

I was scheduled to leave Hong Kong in mid-August, which would give me a few weeks to settle in before classes started at USC.

"It's cheaper here," my mother said, taking me shopping to make sure I had enough clothes and necessities. "If you stock up as much as you can, you won't have to buy a lot in Los Angeles."

She didn't tell me how she felt about my leaving. She didn't express pride that I was going overseas for an advanced degree, one of only three female graduates who had such an opportunity. We talked about clothes. We talked about *The Young Lions*, *Some Like It Hot*, *North by Northwest*—all the latest movies. But every time she came into my room to see how my packing was getting along, she cried. I had seen her cry so often—when Ngoi-Gung scolded, when she felt helpless with my father—that I didn't usually pay any attention; it was one of her default states. But this was different. She was crying for me, because she didn't want me to leave. I became confused. Her physical punishment, her nagging, her rejection of my early attempts at affection and reconciliation, her threats to disown me—I couldn't count how often she'd made me cry, showing no sympathy or remorse. And now...? Was she sad about losing me? Was she frustrated at feeling powerless, at the prospect of losing a person subordinate to her? Or did my expansive prospects remind her of how narrow hers had become?

I told her that I was pushing up my departure date to the end of July.

"Why do you have to change your schedule?" she asked. "Can't you go as planned? Au-Yeung's not leaving until the end of August."

I didn't confess my reason: that each day I didn't leave was one in which anything could happen to prevent me from *ever* leaving, and I wouldn't feel safe in my commitment until I was across the Pacific.

A week after I changed my plane reservation, I overheard my mother talking to Bess, her voice quavering.

"I don't understand why she hates her family so much," she complained and started to sob.

I marched into the room. "That's all you know how to do. Can't you stop crying for once and say something?"

My hostility was at odds with what was going on inside me. I wanted to hug her, to comfort her, but I couldn't forget what had happened the one time I'd tried. *You can visit me whenever you please*, I had the urge to say, but honestly, I didn't know whether I liked or disliked her. Why had she never said she loved me? Did she think it wasn't necessary because mothers naturally love their children? Maybe it wasn't important if she loved me. Maybe it was more important that I loved her. But why couldn't I find the words?

Floundering in my amorphous, unsettled feelings, I scoffed, "Can't you stop crying?" and this of course made her cry all the more.

I wish I hadn't been so mean, but standing there while her tears fell and Bess needlessly rearranged clothes in my suitcase, it was easier to deny my gentler feelings than to misinterpret and hope.

Asian. It wasn't how Reiko or I ever described ourselves *to ourselves*. I was Chinese. She was Japanese. But as soon as we arrived in America, we had become something else. It was the same for any immigrant from Vietnam, the Philippines, Cambodia, Korea. Our national identities, let alone our regional ones, were gone. We had all become simply, reductively *Asian*. If the organization that Reiko and I were working to create—Asian Community Mental Health Services—was to be successful, it would have to break "Asian" into its constituent parts and treat patients in ways that, while likely new to them, were not dismissive of their heritage.

We attended seminars on proposal writing and community engagement. We established a board to advise and oversee our organization, even before it technically existed. We addressed a county supervisors' meeting, speaking pointedly about an issue I'd touched on in my Chinese Family Outreach proposal: that there was no preventive care for Asian immigrants; while the ER was a last resort for most people, a place to visit rarely, if ever, it was the first and only resort for Asians, which was quite costly to taxpayers.

The groundwork laid, Reiko and I wrote our proposal, citing the Chinese Family Outreach Program as proof of concept. We secured funding from Alameda County and several family foundations, and ACMHS came into existence.

With my responsibilities for the Outreach Program and the new organization, I started working full time. And as was unfortunately typical in the early days of such efforts, we relied heavily on volunteers. We didn't care whether they were trained or not so long as they offered what I'll call cultural expertise. Chinese, Japanese, Vietnamese, Filipino, Cambodian, Korean—it wasn't easy to find people. Some of our volunteers were newly arrived immigrants themselves, the kind that the Council helped with finances and employment.

In the mid 1970s, as the war in Southeast Asia ground to an end, there was an influx of refugees from Vietnam. Chung was one of these. He'd been studying to become a lawyer back home, but I hired him as a Mental Health Specialist, despite his lack of experience, because he could speak Vietnamese. He wound up working for the county for three decades. His career enabled him to buy a house, raise his children, and send them to college. One of his sons became the lawyer that he had never been.

"Thank you," he said to me nearly twenty years after I met him. "Thank you for giving me a chance."

I understand how someone might find it disorienting, that a few organizations I'd either founded or co-founded, but didn't run, existed concurrently. I want to be clear: I was never an *employee* of the Chinese Community Council, Family Outreach Program, or Asian Community Mental Health Services; I remained, throughout, employed by the International Institute of East Bay.

In its second year, the Outreach Program was still under the auspices of the Institute, although it was funded by the Department of Mental Hygiene. For it to survive into a third year, and for economic reasons, the state required that it merge with another organization. Since all of my cases at that time were Chinese, I deemed the Chinese Community Council the best fit, and I met with Cecilia, its Director, to discuss a merger. She flatly refused.

"You'll try to take over," she said.

If I wanted to be head of the Council, I didn't say, *I already would be*. I saw it time and again, how ego often took hold once people reached a certain level, how they became more concerned with protecting their territory and power than promoting the general welfare.

In the end—a new beginning—the Outreach Program folded into Asian Community Mental Health Services, which operated out of an Episcopalian church in Oakland's Chinatown. Yes, one organization that I, an employee of the International Institute, had founded was subsumed into another that I had co-founded. Disorienting? The unsteady financial ground that underlies social service programs forces them to do whatever it takes to survive.

With my last semester at Chung Chi winding down, the Dean of Registration asked to see me. I thought something must be wrong. Didn't I have enough credits to graduate?

"Please, sit," he said and gestured at a chair facing his desk.

He was big for a Chinese, a heavy-set man who inevitably had to warm into movement, and he had a booming voice. We called him the Coal Burning Bus because such buses always made loud noises and required a crank to start their engines. He sat looking at me with a serious expression but a smile about his lips.

"You have been chosen as the female valedictorian of your graduating class," he said.

Me, a valedictorian? I couldn't possibly have deserved it. No way was I going to stand at a podium and speak in front of a crowd.

"I'm sorry, but I decline being a valedictorian," I said.

Coal Burning Bus frowned. "It's not a matter of choice. This is an assignment. You were chosen and it's an honor."

"I understand, but I don't want it. Maybe somebody else would like to have the honor?"

Coal Burning Bus became angry. "No one ever refuses! People hope for this recognition!"

I didn't know what to say.

"Listen." He wheezed into a lower gear. "You'll shortly be going out to face the world and you must learn to be gracious and accept responsibility. And if you don't accept, you won't graduate with your class."

"What if I become ill?"

"Then you must have a doctor's certificate proving it, but you will still have to write a valedictory speech. And if you really *are* ill," he gave me a dubious look, "I will ask another student to read it, because if you become ill so close to graduation, no one else will have time to write their own."

From that interview until graduation was the most miserable time of my entire college career. All I could think about was how to get out of giving my speech, and I prayed constantly, *God, Guanyin, please strike me low*. Unfortunately, I had never been healthier.

On stage in my cap and gown, with a stomach full of moths (I don't get butterflies), I sat drenched in a nervous sweat while the chaplain spoke, followed by the President of the college, and then the Coal Burning Bus, each saying whatever he said to the audience of 150 students, their parents and guests. As my turn approached, I tried to calm down by remembering that I was just going to read what I'd written, and I knew how to read, didn't I? This didn't help me feel any calmer, as far as I could tell, but it worked because I somehow made my way to the microphone and heard my voice sail out over the crowd.

Now that we are embarking on new adventures in life, let us not forget that each of us has a responsibility for the well-being of others. We are fortunate, as so few people in Hong Kong have the advantage of a college education. Therefore, the burden—the privilege—is on us to be the leaders of social change, and for every blessing we receive, let us give back to society in greater measure.

I went on to talk about how Hong Kong, given the number of refugees coming in every day, could be an example to the rest of the world in terms of resourcefulness and compassion. And I concluded by encouraging my classmates to leap into the coming decade with vitality and enthusiasm, to let idealism inspire but not blind, so that we might all attain our dreams while making the world a more humane place.

"You started off shaky," my mother said afterward, "but once you got going, you were fine."

Coal Burning Bus congratulated me. "I knew you could do it!"

That night, my parents hosted a dinner in my honor. But surrounded by well-wishing adults—and for no reason I understood, surprised by my own sentimentality and nostalgia—I found myself thinking of the Komsomol, of my weekly rendezvous in the cemetery with Chui, whom I had suspected was a spy for our unnamed superiors. Hadn't Chui and I been friends, beyond our kinship over the common goal of wanting to liberate the suffering masses? Probably not, but it seemed so to me, in retrospect, and I missed her. I felt a greater loss over Mrs. Tang, however, who had recruited me to the Communist cause. My feelings toward her weren't as mixed as they had been when I left Macau and didn't know if she liked me for myself or only saw me as a tool for the Komsomol. She had never responded to the letter I'd sent, in which I explained why I was quitting the Communist Youth group. Was she disappointed in me? Did she blame herself for choosing me as a youth leader? Did she think of me *at all*?

I glanced around at the smiling faces of my parents. Was I brave enough to go to America and leave the only support system I'd ever known, as rickety as it had been? So many people suffered pain and unhappiness. So many people, longing for change, made an escape that didn't turn out to be an escape in the least. Was I doing that? Alex was still a possibility, I thought, but if not...well, the local job market was wide open to me, and I could have my own little flat and a day-time maid. I could continue to serve the refugees of Hong Kong, gaining all the real-world experience I was able to handle. After a few years, MSW degrees might be offered by Chung Chi or HKU.

My mother's voice rose above the general din—a flutter of laughter.

I was about to throw away my baby bottle for a cup. Although I had wanted to throw that bottle away for years, now that I was to take hold of the cup, I instinctively recoiled toward my bottle. But if I clung to the familiar, I reminded myself, I might well be miserable; the familiar was unsatisfactory, lacking, and I would leave the question *What if I had only...?* forever open. So I had to go.

Yet I'd do one thing before I left Hong Kong: visit Macau and talk to Mrs. Tang face-to-face. Regardless of her motivation, I wanted to express my appreciation for her interest in me, her dedication and care, and to apologize if I had let her down or caused her the slightest hardship. But I also needed to prove that our time together had been real. Because our afternoons studying, our evening meals with her daughter, her invitation to join the Komsomol—it all seemed to have happened to somebody else, a character in a story or dream.

11

MY PARENTS VISITED THE STATES in the fall of 1977. My father was suffering from colon cancer. The colostomy bags he used weren't well made and often smelled, which greatly embarrassed him. I took him to a medical supply store and bought him the best bags I could find.

With shy hope in his voice, he told me, "Some friends of mine in Hong Kong, who have children in the US, they said you will ask me to stay here."

I shook my head. "I'm sorry, De-Di, but I can't. Steve and I would have to be your sponsor and guarantee that you won't become a financial liability to the government. We're not in a position to do that yet."

Disappointed, he and my mother returned to Hong Kong, where doctors discovered that his cancer had metastasized to his lungs. The prognosis was dire.

He hoped to see Bentham one last time, and not just because he loved his son; Bentham was a *doctor*. No matter that he wasn't an oncologist; being a doctor was enough for my father to want his professional opinion regarding treatment options. But the

Communists wouldn't let Bentham visit, worried that my father's illness was a ploy for a man of much-needed skill on the mainland to get out from under their regime.

My father died of cancer in the spring of 1979. At his funeral, guilt overwhelmed me. If I had agreed to sponsor him, he might have received better medical care in the States. Something might have been done to save him.

Bentham was not allowed to attend the funeral. Not until underground Communists in Hong Kong saw our father's obituary in the newspaper and informed the mainland was he trusted to travel. He arrived in Hong Kong to participate in the scattering of our father's ashes at a cove on Finley Road—a ceremony I would miss, as I was heading back to California. But that's when I saw my brother again, between the funeral and the scattering of ashes. Not quite as tall or lanky as he used to be, he was a graying middle-aged man. I liked to think the years had been kinder to me. We didn't talk much, given the occasion and that a lot had happened to each of us in the other's absence, but he remained committed to the people's cause and told me that he had tried and failed three times to become a full-fledged member of the Communist Party.

After four years as a naval officer, Steve was back in the private sector, working first at the architecture firm Welton Becket & Associates—Mr. Becket had designed the Capitol Records building in Los Angeles—then at Pierre & Associates. The racism persisted: he didn't clean toilets or fetch coffee, but—

"I don't want to spend my life drawing other people's ideas," he said.

Through his employment, he met an ambitious, well-connected man named Burton, who told him that the San Francisco Board of Education was looking to hire a Planner, which paid more than he was making. Government jobs were considered the most secure and often sought by immigrants.

"The golden rice bowl," I said, hearing about it.

With two children now—our PERT chart had undergone a few revisions—Steve applied for the position and got it. But this particular rice bowl wasn't *that* golden. Even with his increased salary, it seemed impossible we could ever become millionaires on our combined income, despite being disciplined budgeters for whom no amount of savings was too small.

But as Steve was toiling his way up to Director of School Maintenance, Burton approached us about investing with him and a few others in a six-unit apartment building in San Francisco's Marina District, a prime location. Our shares in the business would be determined by the amount of our contribution. Steve and I had amassed a modest nest egg by then and we decided to risk it, taking turns with Burton and our partners as the building superintendent. The property increased in value, and with Burton spearheading the decisions, we sold it and used the proceeds to buy another building. The value of *that* increased, and our little consortium refinanced it instead of putting it on the market, cashing out a chunk of equity that we used to buy another rental property. We did this again and again—sometimes selling a building at a profit, other times refinancing and owning a few buildings at a time—until a day finally came...

Steve was at his computer, looking over our accounts and investments, our PERT chart spread out on his desk. All of a sudden he flumped back in his chair with a stunned look on his face.

"What?" I asked.

He remained wide-eyed but his lips spread into a grin. He tapped at the papers in front of him, and I knew. We didn't have a million dollars in cash, but we had done it, had reached a level of economic security, of net worth, that hadn't seemed realistically achievable. Of course, in many US cities these days, families living middle-class lives are technically millionaires because housing is so expensive. But for me and Steve, "technically" wasn't a disparaging or minimizing term; what we had done would allow us greater freedom to shape the next phase of our lives and provide our girls with a solid economic foundation on which to build, whatever their aspirations.

Soon after, we were on a family trip to Newport, Rhode Island, showing our daughters the Officer Candidate School and telling them about our time there. We stopped for dinner at the seafood restaurant that had been the candidates' weekend haunt back when Steve was in training, but which he had never set foot in for lack of money. It was nothing like the cheap Chinese place we had occasionally treated ourselves to over the past decades. Steve ordered lobster, and I suppose he worked up quite an appetite, cracking open claws and legs, because when his plate held nothing but spent shells, he did something he had never done before—gestured for the waiter and ordered seconds, another lobster.

"She still teaches junior high. Her daughter's in high school," a friend in Macau told me over the phone.

I planned a day-trip to say goodbye to Mrs. Tang. But the night before I was to travel by hydrofoil, my friend called.

"She went to Canton to visit her parents for ten days."

Ten days! I would be in my last week in Hong Kong, wrapping up my preparations and sitting for my final interviews at the American Consulate. Why had I waited so long to try and see Mrs. Tang? Why hadn't I visited her the previous summer or during Chinese New Year?

"If you hadn't changed your travel date from August to July," my mother sniffed, "you could have seen your favorite teacher one last time."

Asian Community Mental Health Services had been in operation for about two years, and I was still working at the International Institute of East Bay, when a Deputy Director of Mental Health for the county pursued me for a psychiatric social worker position. Wouldn't I like to make a positive impact at the county level, as far as services for Asians were concerned? I would. I accepted the job and worked at an outpatient clinic in downtown Oakland, mostly with Cantonese-speaking Chinese patients, many of whom came to me for therapy as a condition of being discharged from psych wards. And any time an Asian entered the county system, the paperwork was sent to me, and I arranged proper treatment for them.

One patient, a schizophrenic, had recently come to the States and made a living selling his paintings on the streets of San Francisco. The problem was, whenever he put brush to canvas, he would have an episode. He bonded with me because we were both from Hong Kong. I got him on medication and he had to stop painting. Stabilized, he was able to stay home and care for his young son while his wife worked. I counseled him for fifteen years.

"I'd like to paint a picture for you," he said at one of our last sessions, when I told him I was retiring.

"You can't. You'll have a relapse."

"It's okay," he said. "I really want to."

I couldn't stop him, it seemed, so I gave him a photograph of a house in Lake Tahoe that Steve and I owned, along with samples of local foliage. Using these, he painted a landscape, a subtle portrait of our part-time home that still hangs above my mantel—and he didn't have an episode.

As years passed, I directed both Alameda County's Asian program and a "central" team, which served anyone who came in the door. Like the wealthy heiress who lived off stock she had inherited and slashed her wrists every year to get her parents' attention. Like the white woman in her thirties who'd gone out of her way to have a child with a black man because her mother had always told her the child would undoubtedly be cute, and also mixed blood had benefits—although she, my patient, couldn't put into words what those benefits were.

I organized an Asian-American County Mental Health Employee Caucus, regularly bringing together Asians and Pacific Islanders who worked in various departments. I believed it was—and is—important to open doors for our phenotype in the social services field.

"Intelligent, competent people who look like us should not restrict themselves to the Asian community," I would remind the caucus. "They are capable of bringing their talents to the greater community and the benefit of all."

My responsibilities for Alameda County, and the fact that we shared funding for program activities like picnics, made me a sort of unofficial liaison with ACMHS. From this position, over the years, I watched as the organization I had co-founded became increasingly bureaucratic. But I never would have guessed that one day, long after my time—long after my retirement and Steve's death, in fact—ACMHS would fall victim to its own missteps, with rampant political infighting among board members and a fatal lack of communication between the board and staff. Its Director, an architect ill-equipped for the position, would eventually be discovered to have misused funds, spending them to renovate the waiting area instead of hiring social workers and psychiatrists, as he was supposed to do, and the county would close ACMHS.

Mismanagement born of ineptitude, egotism, and politics. A general lack of effectiveness. These seem to be viruses common to unwieldy bureaucracies. At the county level, their virulence was astonishing. After sixteen years, I was discouraged, exhausted.

"What have you been saying so often lately?" Steve asked. "In order to change larger society, we need to produce citizens who can effect change at local levels."

"The academic world shouldn't be an ivory tower, but more integrated with communities," I said.

"Right."

"Less a matter of intellectual exercises in a classroom and more direct action."

"Right. And what good is our financial freedom if we don't make the most of it?"

So we both retired, gave up our not-so-golden rice bowls. Steve had thoughts of becoming an entrepreneur, importing steel salvaged from old PT boats into China. I was determined to be as active as ever in my efforts to assist those in need—by volunteering and consulting the Asian Pacific Fund to identify organizations worthy of donations. Then Steve got sick.

I'd be leaving for California in a week. My mother insisted we do yet another round of shopping, and it was while we were out one afternoon that it happened. Nothing momentous occurred to provoke it—my looming departure, I suppose, enough for me to see her with some emotional detachment. She was musing aloud to a merchant about the stitching of a handbag, which was her way of haggling, and I had a glimpse of her untainted by defensiveness, resentment, or hostility. I had always believed that her obsession with shopping meant she was shallow and stupid. But it *was* a talent, and an indication of much more than I, in my adolescent arrogance, had thought. She could get anyone to feel comfortable, to open up and talk. Hadn't I witnessed it countless times at those ice cream parties she used to host—how accommodating and encouraging she could be with her fellow Ginling alumnae, all of whom seemed to admire her? And at the local shops, her easygoing manner...I was about to call it natural-*seeming*, but no, in those instances, I think it was natural, her easygoing manner so genuine and engaging that she inevitably got bargains on good-quality items without vendors feeling squeezed. That day while she chatted with the merchant, praising and subtly critiquing the handbag almost in the same breath, I saw her as a person in her own right: a woman who had experienced happiness and disappointment in life; a daughter who wasn't her parents' favorite; a wife who had little rapport with her husband; a mother whose son had left her and whose daughter was about to do the same. I might not have felt overly affectionate toward her, but as she settled on the handbag's price, I regretted that once I left, the chance to truly know her would be lost.

I must be very apprehensive about my trip if I'm trying to cling to my mother, I thought. When I'm in America, I'll write her a letter. I'll start it with "My Dearest Mom" and sign it "Love, Ret."

That letter was never written.

I last saw my mother in Beijing, in November of 1985—one of the few times we talked without argument or tears. She died two months afterward and I didn't return for her funeral.

"Too late!" she'd yelled when she had kicked me, a seven-year-old, out of the Canton flat.

It was true all of our lives.

My father was especially quiet, intent on his games of solitaire, those final days. As I've said, this was a sign that his finances weren't in great shape. I didn't yet have enough experience to know if his refusal to talk about money with the women in his life was a trait of Chinese men or of men in general. But my parents' strictly defined roles in the household had always bothered me, and I swore that when I was married, I would do things differently. There would be no power struggle between me and my husband to determine who was the breadwinner, who the homemaker. No such dichotomy would exist; we would share all responsibilities as equally as we could.

"Make the most of this opportunity and learn as much as you can," my father said, looking up from his cards. "Studying well is your duty. Ensuring the money's there to support your education is mine."

He didn't mention his older brother Wu, who lived in San Francisco, or his younger brother Chung in Fresno, neither of whom I'd met. Instead, he talked about his time at Cornell thirty years earlier, and the professors who had graded students on the basis of how much they liked them. Then he returned to his lonely card game.

"I will send the necessary amount so that you won't have to work, unless you choose to get some job experience during the summer," he said—the closest he ever came to expressing his feelings about my impending absence.

How could I tell if a professor liked me or not? At Chung Chi, Chinese professors expected quiet, studious students while the Europeans preferred students to challenge them, which had proven awkward, since Chinese culture insisted on quiet respect for a teacher's wisdom and authority. The missionary lady who had taught English Conversation and was under the mistaken impression that Hong Kong's humidity would somehow air out the room—I think she wasn't fond of me so much as merely appreciative that I opened the window at the start of every class. Were she or Mrs. Finske, with whom I'd clashed over the assignment on the Old and New Testaments, typical examples of what I'd find in American classrooms? They seemed to respect me. But like me? I wasn't so sure.

At USC, I was too overwhelmed by the magnitude of overall change to worry about where I stood in professors' affections. The university was huge compared to Chung Chi, its architecture intimidating, its students—all of them sure-footed—daunting in number. In addition, the sprawl of Los Angeles itself was hard to comprehend, and I failed the school's English proficiency test, administered in my first week. I had passed the one required by the embassy, but USC's test made cultural assumptions I didn't understand. *If you are on the northeast corner of Figueroa Street and you turn right, will you be facing the northwest corner or the southeast corner or...?* This was an unfamiliar way of thinking to me. I spent two weeks in Remedial English, instead of the expected semester, before I passed the required test and was allowed to pursue my social work curriculum.

The majority of my classmates were already well established in the field—Managers and Directors with decades or more of experience behind them. They had taken leave from their jobs in order to get an MSW, which hadn't been offered when they were younger. Apparently, an increasing number of their new hires had MSWs, and it didn't look good for entry-level staff to have more advanced degrees than they themselves had. Plus, the National Association of Social Work was beginning to formulate requirements for certification, to ensure a standard of care in the profession.

So my classmates, much older and more seasoned than I, had an easier time discussing *practice*. This, for me, was problematic because lessons weren't strictly lectures during which I quietly took notes or even occasionally questioned the material; they were more of a discussion. Naturally shy in new situations, my relative lack of experience compared to other students rendered me more so, and I never raised my hand or even made eye contact with professors. I had a hard time paying attention, afraid of being sounded for my thoughts on a topic, or, in one class, asking why everyone was talking about peanut envy and how it could manifest in children as early as five and six years old.

"Penis," my advisor corrected later. "*Penis envy.*"

Peanut, penis—no matter, I still didn't want to speak in class. My advisor talked with my professors and they agreed not to call on me.

"When I have something to say, I'll say it," I had promised my advisor.

I never did, though, and I often sat in class with discussions raging around me, wondering, What kind of professor keeps asking students for their thoughts, never authoritatively stating facts?

My father now spent more time shuffling his deck of cards than dealing them out for solitaire. My mother came in and out of the flat with newly bought clothes that I didn't have room for in my suitcases. Ngoi-Po paced her room, complaining about the heat. Ah Ying confessed to me that she didn't think she would still be working for my family by the time I returned; Grandpa Ho was getting to be too much for her.

"But my parents need you," I said. "Please stay and look after them for me."

She said she would try and gave me a pink sleeveless summer blouse as a going-away present.

I myself hadn't said a word to Ngoi-Gung in three years, my anger toward him as fresh as the day he'd brandished a knife at me. I told my mother that I wouldn't return to Hong Kong as long as he was alive.

"But he's eighty-seven. This might be the last time you see him," she said, urging me to talk to him.

"I will say goodbye the morning I leave," I promised. "I don't want to risk an unpleasant scene by acknowledging him before then."

Grateful, she smiled and, turning away so that I wouldn't see her cry, told Ah Ying to sew a small inner pocket in my undershirt, where I could keep my money safe while I traveled.

The day finally arrived. My alarm went off at three in the morning. I don't know how to describe my feelings other than to say I wasn't exactly happy or excited; I was contained, detached. I dressed in a new gray skirt and the sleeveless blouse Ah Ying had given me, then shuffled out of my room. To my surprise, Ngoi-Gung was already awake, sitting in his usual spot on the living room sofa, next to the radio on the windowsill. I didn't acknowledge him and ate my breakfast. Ah Ying had gotten up early to make my favorite meal—rice porridge with minced beef and Chinese tomatoes, and for once I didn't mind eating so much first thing.

Ngoi-Po emerged from her room and wished me success in my studies. "I doubt you'll see me again," she said sadly.

"What are you talking about?" I countered, knowing that she badly wanted to visit her daughter in America but had never been invited. "As soon as I can afford to, I'll send a ticket for you to come see me at Auntie Lily's house!"

My parents appeared. My father didn't say a word. My mother of course started crying, which got Ah Ying crying, and then—me too. It was horrible: nothing but silence from some, sniffles and sobs from the rest of us.

I went back to my room, to sit alone for a while. I slid a box out from under my bed, which contained items of sentimental value I wouldn't be taking with me, and I said goodbye to Yung-Yung, the old doll my godfather had given me when we first moved to Macau.

Bess's Shanghainese boyfriend, who was driving me to the airport, rang the doorbell at five-thirty. Bess had clung to this young man; worried about becoming an old maid as she was, she would likely become his wife. Realizing this, Au-Yeung and I had stopped trying to get her to dump him.

"Bring along a sweater," my mother advised while Ah Ying gathered my suitcases together.

I had two carry-ons, one containing *The Arabian Nights*, a camera, beef jerky, chewing gum, binoculars, and the sweater. The other was my handbag with its "questionable" stitching. It held my passport, airline ticket, address book, and just enough money to keep any thieves I might encounter from searching me further.

I hugged Ngoi-Po and turned to see Ngoi-Gung standing up, facing my direction. My mother gestured for me to approach him. I embraced him and, to my surprise, felt his tears on my shoulder.

"Don't stay too long now," he said brokenly. "Be sure you come back."

He took a US fifty-dollar bill from his pocket and gave it to me. Even back when he'd been rich, he had never given anybody money. Where he'd gotten fifty American dollars, a significant sum in those days, I had no idea.

"Take care," I said.

He sobbed outright, and with a shock I realized that this tyrannical old grouch, this man I hated, had warm feelings for me.

I wish I could say that I immediately relaxed toward him, that I had something of an epiphany and understood his crusty, hypercritical manner to be a defensive result of the poverty and racism he'd lived through. But I didn't. Not then. Not until after he died, in 1966, in the North Point flat. Not until I was in my first year of motherhood, when Maa-Mi called and told me that his ashes had been scattered off the docks, did I find love and forgiveness for Ngoi-Gung in my heart.

He was still sobbing. My grandmother came up beside me.

"The old man loves you," she said. "He just has a stiff mouth," meaning that he couldn't say it.

Mine, a family of stiff-mouths.

At Kai Tak Airport, Bess's boyfriend parked the car and took pictures of me with my parents and Ah Ying, but I don't recall us actually saying goodbye. Suddenly I was in a window seat on the plane, my handbag in my lap. Through my little window I saw a few silver clouds drifting in a bright blue sky. My parents and Ah Ying, who knew what row I was in, were standing behind the chain-link fence, waving at my plane. I waved back. The plane started forward, thrumming. The cabin rumbled, shook, and then—

Lightness. We were up and away, soaring toward the clouds.

I tried to get a last look at Hong Kong, but my tears blurred everything.

"Leaving home for the first time?" the middle-aged gentleman next to me said, somewhere between a question and quiet acknowledgment of a fact.

I must have answered him, but all I remember is that, as the plane angled higher and higher, I thought, *Well, that's it then. I'm on my way to America.*

No wish-granting genie comes with a magic carpet. It carries you to a land you have long dreamed of, but which—initially, at least—disappoints because it isn't a paradise. In many ways, it resembles the place you left, and you have to work harder than ever, striving and striving.

Steve, before you died, I asked you to forgive me for whatever I had done wrong or not enough of in our life together, and you said without hesitation that you did. You know that I have always felt I would fulfill an important mission. I don't think I've fulfilled it yet. So I must learn to live—borrowing, through remembrance, from your strength and courage. I will always grieve your loss, but everything I do from now on will be a celebration of what we accomplished together. I am fortunate in my economic security. I can use whatever money I'm able to spare to help those most vulnerable and in need. Yes, I must go on trying—volunteering at the Hong Fook Center and donating to impactful charities researched through the Asian Pacific Fund; but especially, by funding projects at USC's School of Social Work, and by collaborating with its Office of Advancement, with department heads and professors, to effect positive change in how students are taught. Because classroom discussions about theory and practice are not enough. MSW candidates need to have a greater dialogue with communities—only this way, I believe, can one learn to be flexible in one's approach to specific social and mental health problems, allowing for idiosyncrasies of method in both outreach and treatment. People are more than case studies. My work of improving mental health care for Asian-Americans, and for marginalized populations in general, must continue.

Earlier, I said that everyone has a magic carpet and the trick is to recognize it, to find the courage to pilot it. I still believe that, very much so, and yet…I've had it wrong all this time, haven't I? Imagining I could sail off and leave the past behind? My magic carpet ride is ongoing. I have always been on it, and although it's often felt earth-bound, as crowded with failures and disillusionment as with victories and elation, that hasn't made it any less magical.

AFTERWORD

THREE YEARS AFTER STEVE DIED, I met Paul, his best friend's older brother. A retired engineer who had worked at Hughes Aircraft for nearly four decades, Paul had four adult children—two sons and two daughters—and he'd lost his wife twelve months earlier. Like me, he'd been married for thirty-five years. Losing long-term spouses at that stage in our lives, we developed a powerful bond that, in time, matured into much more. We married in 2009, weaving together our magic carpets, and have since traveled the world, visiting all seven continents and over eighty countries.

Paul is a man of integrity, patience, and generosity. I am grateful to have him in my life.

ACKNOWLEDGMENTS

In deep appreciation and gratitude...

Zoe Borkowski, a mentor who taught me so much, not least about myself, and helped me grow from from a shy family social case worker into a community activist.

Dede Huang, my cousin, whose support and encouragement was indispensable from the moment she heard about my desire to write a memoir, and who tracked down family photos of me and my parents that I thought had long been lost.

Rodger Lum and Reiko True, my former colleagues and co-workers, for their personal support throughout my career, and for their efforts in helping to establish and develop social and mental health services for Asian communities in the Greater East Bay.

Beth Logan, whose encouragement and empathy helped me find an inner strength and the confidence to take on the huge commitment of writing a memoir.

And last but not least, Eric Laster, whose talent and skill shaped the seemingly disconnected episodes of my life into this book.

ABOUT THE AUTHORS

Loretta Taam lives in Northern California. Through her philanthropy, she continues to improve access to quality social services and mental health care for all. She also collaborates with the USC Office of Advancement and Suzanne Dworak-Peck School of Social Work to ensure that, for future MSWs, theoretical considerations do not override dialogue with community members. This is her first book.

Eric Laster lives in Los Angeles where, in addition to penciling fiction, he provides strategic writing services to select clients. For many years, he worked as a *New York Times* best-selling ghostwriter. He is the admitted author of two books for middle graders, *Welfy Q. Deederhoth: Meat Purveyor, World Savior* and The *Adventures of Erasmus Twiddle*, as well as the novel *Static*. His short fiction has appeared in *Invisible City*, *Southern Humanities Review*, *Epiphany*, *Beloit Fiction Journal*, *Ascent*, and elsewhere.